▷ "Two of the more pronounced voids in many youth ministries today are a strategic plan for discipleship and an intentional effort to provide opportunities for one-on-one mentoring/coaching. This book will greatly help any youth leader in the realization of both of those values. By being Christ-centered and calling for radical change, this book strikes the right balance between the call to 'be' and call to 'do.' Combine that with a spiritual coach and you're done just talking about making disciples...you're doing it."

—**David Hertweck**, District Youth Director,
New York District of the Assemblies of God (www.nydag.org)

LEARNING TO FOLLOW JESUS

youth edition

by Daniel McNaughton and
Claude Valdes, Jr.

www.learningtofollow.net

Morning Joy Media
Spring City, Pennsylvania

Portions excerpted by permission from *Learning to Follow Jesus* by Daniel McNaughton.

Published by Morning Joy Media.

Visit www.morningjoymedia.com for more information on bulk discounts and special promotions, or e-mail your questions to info@morningjoymedia.com.

Design: Meredith Valdes
Author Photos: Dan Desrosiers, Meredith Valdes

Cataloging-In-Publication Data

Subject Headings:
1. Discipling (Christianity) 2. Spiritual formation. 3. Christian life. I. Title.

ISBN 978-1-937107-12-3

Printed in the United States of America

This book is dedicated to my sister, Maralyn Mathias.
Her life, love, and thirst for God inspired me to follow Jesus.

—Daniel McNaughton

To my wife and best friend, Meredith:
Thank you for loving Jesus more than you will ever love me.

—Claude Valdes, Jr.

CONTENTS

(Contents continued...)

ACKNOWLEDGEMENTS

It would be almost impossible for me (Daniel) to list every person who shaped this book, partly because I have a terrible memory and partly because this book has been in the works for so long. I feel like I only played a small role in the formation of this tool. I have borrowed from and have been shaped by so many. I simply wrote what God's people and God's Word said. But I want to try give honor to whom honor is due.

First, I want to give all honor and glory to my precious Lord and Savior Jesus Christ, through whom and for whom everything has been written.

I am deeply grateful for my wife and closest friend, Amy. She has read, reread, edited and critiqued the entire work many times. Her attention to detail has made this work much better work than it would have been without her.

I am grateful for my father, Eldon McNaughton, who inspires me by his life and his words to follow Jesus. He and his wife, Kay, have read every word of this manuscript, prayed daily for me, and continually encouraged me throughout the project. The rest of my immediate family has provided immeasurable encouragement, suggestions and prayer throughout this project. Several of them carefully read the manuscript and provided helpful advice: Ron & Donna McNaughton, Jim & Maralyn Mathias, Judd McNaughton and Sherri Stapleton.

This book grew out of authentic Christian community. The impetus for this book came out of a strategic planning team meeting at Spring Valley Community Church (Barry Behnke, Lee Bilotta,

Jonathan Capeci, Dick Gruber, and Joe Terreri). We heard from God together, and they encouraged and commissioned me to write this book. I would probably still be saying “someday” if it were not for them.

An unexpected blessing was seeing God launch the publishing ministry of Debbie Capeci and Morning Joy Media through this project. I discovered her passion for publishing about the time I decided to write. The inside design [of the adult version] is all hers. She has given me countless suggestions to make this project better.

Many friends have read, worked through, and shaped various forms of this work. Hundreds of students in my Introduction to Christian Living classes at Valley Forge Christian College sharpened me and challenged me to explore a discipleship paradigm that was Jesus-focused, story-based, and practical.

I am grateful for my dear friend, Pastor Bryan Koch and Glad Tidings Assembly of God Church (www.gtaog.org). He has walked with me throughout this process and is leading the way, demonstrating how larger churches can implement this tool.

More recently the Spiritual Coaches Training groups have given me invaluable suggestions as well: Jim & Sue-Ellen Edmonds, Heather Cosme, Barbara Behnke, Nina Morales, Dave & Janie Oehlert, Kim Ortiz, Jennifer Olson, Marie Sabatelli, and Faith Saunders. Several individuals also gave me fresh perspectives: Loretta Roberts, Chris Brander, Paul McGonigle, and Steve Clerico.

Finally, I am humbled and thankful for the community of believers at Spring Valley Community Church whose lives and passion to follow Jesus continually spur me on. This book is truly a community effort. To God be the glory!

—Daniel McNaughton

I (Claude) have been incredibly humbled throughout this entire project. *Learning to Follow Jesus: Youth Edition* is clearly a God thing. I have never been so obviously and unmistakably able to take zero credit for something than I am for what is on the following pages. I would classify writing as one of my greatest weaknesses. I am weak but he is strong! I have surrendered my life to following him, and I'm thankful that he has leveraged my life for his glory.

I must first acknowledge Jesus Christ; he laid his life down for me while I was still an enemy of God. His continual love and patience towards me brings me to tears as I write this. He is my everything.

Dr. Daniel McNaughton deserves any and all credit for the foundation of the content of this resource. He is passionate about making disciples and following Jesus. He was my spiritual coach before either of us knew what that meant! I am thankful that he had a vision for a youth edition and invited me to be a part of what God was clearly doing. He has impacted my life in ways he may never know.

I can't even begin to appropriately acknowledge my wife, best friend and biggest fan, Meredith. She has designed this entire work, from front to back (including the front and back)! Her priority on excellence for God's glory is nothing short of inspiring. And she was pregnant with our son through much of this nearly one-year project! She is a godly, strong, woman of integrity, and I am thankful that our two precious girls, Ellise and Aubree, can watch her model what it is to follow Jesus.

I must acknowledge my parents, Claude and Laura Valdes, as well as my in-laws, David and Jeanne Wessman. We stand on their shoulders. I am so thankful that Meredith and I have witnessed first-hand what following Jesus looks like in the lives of our parents!

David Hertweck has been a true lifeline, walking alongside me in this journey. He is an authentic follower of Jesus with a passion for discipleship and youth ministry. He and three others joined me to be watchful, Christ-centered, youth-passionate eyes and voices throughout this project: Mike Becher, Rob Kirk, and Jeremiah Poulsen. I am grateful to call them friends. Their contribution has been clearly eternal. Joining these original four, Justin Adour, Jimmy Armpriester, Joshua Hamlin, Dave Leandre, Donnie Marsh, and Charles Moodie agreed to be beta sites. Their insight and grass roots feedback has been priceless in the shaping of this resource. Along with those ten, the following rounded out the first wave of youth spiritual coaches: Kevin Bateman, Amy Davis, Daniel Dedrick, Mark Freeman, Doug Hammack, Manny Marin, John Pelkey, Edwin Sechrist and Brandon Scholes. The way in which each of these nineteen individuals gave of their time and energy in order to create an environment where teenagers could learn to follow Jesus is nothing short of biblical! Thank you.

The publisher, Debbie Capeci of Morning Joy Media, is so much more than a publisher. She has been a supporter and fan of what God has been doing from the moment this project began. Her contribution is immeasurable. Thank you also to the many editors and proofreaders that caught things my eyes simply do not see!

Finally, in so many ways we are shaped by those with whom we follow Jesus. Word of Life AG has shaped me; thank you for desiring to follow Jesus! I dare not mention one staff member, ministry director, member, or attendee in fear that I will leave a critical one out! I will, however, acknowledge the leader of that wonderful body of Christ followers, Randy Czyz. He is so much more than my senior pastor; he is my friend. He has believed in me in moments when I didn't believe in myself. He released me to create margin in my life so that such a project could be completed. I am deeply grateful that God has permitted me to watch such a wonderful shepherd following Jesus!

—Claude Valdes, Jr.

INTRODUCTION

I (Daniel) will never forget sitting in my office at a church in Toronto, Ontario, where I served as an assistant pastor when it dawned on me that I had never been systematically and intentionally shown how to become a disciple, a fully devoted follower of Jesus. It was shocking to realize the irony. I was raised in a Christian home, attended many Christian meetings, graduated from a denominational college with a degree in Bible, received a master's degree from a reputable seminary, completed more than half of my Ph.D. in Biblical Studies, and was serving as a pastor, but I was never shown how to systematically disciple people. I had invited Christ into my life and was attempting to follow Jesus to the best of my ability, but it was fuzzy. What is a disciple? What does a disciple look like? What does a disciple do?

This was especially disturbing to me because the Gospel of Matthew concludes with the resurrected Jesus appearing to his followers giving them only one command in the Great Commission. It is not "go" as I had often heard preached. It is "make disciples." One command! Why was it fuzzy?

Over the past eighteen years, I have asked many of my friends if they can clearly and succinctly describe what a disciple is and how to make one. Unfortunately, most are like I was...fuzzy. That does not mean we are not making disciples. It is just not clear. Rather than rant about how this could be, I decided to go on a quest to learn how. We cannot change the past, but we can be part of a future that rediscovers what Jesus had in mind when he gave the one command.

This book is designed to be a simple, practical guide for those who want to learn to follow Jesus.

There are three main parts to the guide: a step-by-step development of each quality; resources to augment each quality; and spiritual coaching guides. To get the most out of this book, you will need to read the biblical passages, memorize the Scriptures, write out your answers in the book, pray the prayers, and discuss your progress with a spiritual coach. The goal is not simply to complete the book. The goal is that you will be growing in each of the seven qualities for the rest of your life. When you finish working through the guide one time and are growing in each quality, you are ready to come alongside another person to help him or her learn to follow Jesus. Keep it going! If you help one person a year follow Jesus and if each person you help does the same, and those they help do the same, in thirty-three years we could reach the entire world with the gospel. I want be part of a worldwide movement of people who focus their lives on the "one thing" that matters most to Jesus. How about you?

—Daniel McNaughton

I (Claude) remember in my teenage years trying to figure out so many things. There were daily tensions of wanting to fit in but not being willing to destroy my life in the process. As a result, I was fairly well behaved for all the wrong reasons. I remember being good at some things but at the same time being very aware that there were others that were better, at times feeling alone in a crowded room. Where did I belong? Would anyone truly miss me if I were gone? I had so many questions about so many things. It seemed like no one had any real answers.

I remember truly surrendering to God and deciding to follow him as a teenager. I walked out of a church service that night full of excitement and anticipation. For the first time I thought maybe my life had a bigger purpose. I realized that I was known...by my Creator! I recall asking people "What's next?" The reoccurring answer was "go to youth group." The problem was that although that was important, church attendance had very little impact on me up until that point in my life. I asked people older than myself for advice in how to know God better. The advice I was given over and over was "read your Bible and pray." Good advice, but they felt like boxes to be checked in a long to-do list.

I did the best I could to work through my relationship with God, often having more questions than I did answers. Fast-forward to 1998 (I know...you probably weren't born yet, laugh it up) and I was hired as the youth pastor at Word of Life AG. We immediately started small groups and committed to Christ-centered preaching and teaching. Teenagers started responding to the gospel and lives were being changed. It wasn't too long before a student asked me at the altar with excitement, "So what's next?" In the nearly ten years following that question I purposed to create a disciple-making environment in our youth ministry. From large group to small groups, we were following Jesus together. But there was still a void I struggled to fill: the one-on-one discipleship that also creates healthy accountability for personal time with God. I could only meet with so many students one-on-one. We needed an environment where anyone and everyone had that opportunity...the opportunity to be discipled. It's easy to tell people what they should or need to do. But having them understand why and decide to do it for the right reasons is a different story all together! The tension I was feeling, and what you desire if you are reading this, is the need for what is called a "spiritual coach."

You don't want to follow *that person*, though, because he or she, like you, is simply a sinner saved by grace. No, the only one worth following is Jesus, and a spiritual coach will help you identify the seven qualities of a follower of Jesus that are revealed in the Gospel of Matthew and laid out in the pages of this book. He or she will help create an environment for you to make Christ-centered decisions.

So what's next? Great question! People that meet Jesus want to follow him. *Learning to Follow Jesus: Youth Edition* is what's next! Identify a spiritual coach (if circumstances truly don't allow for you to work with a spiritual coach, this book is designed so that you can self-coach) and get started learning to follow Jesus. The ultimate goal is for you to be growing in the seven qualities from this day forward and, in turn, walking alongside someone else as they learn to follow. That was Jesus' plan...disciples making disciples! There are no more excuses, simply decisions. What will you decide?

—Claude Valdes, Jr.

GETTING STARTED

Congratulations on your decision to follow Jesus! If you have been through *First Steps: Youth Edition* some of "Getting Started" will sound familiar; it's just to ensure that we are all starting at the same point in following Jesus. In fact, you may or may not realize it yet, but accepting the invitation to follow Jesus is the most important decision you will ever make in your life! It will have a positive effect on every decision you'll make as well as where you spend eternity. Your response to God will be life-changing! This book will help you in your walk with Christ so you can know and be known by God the rest of your life and for eternity.

Since it's such an important decision, let's take a few minutes to review what it means to become a follower of Jesus. John 1:12 describes becoming part of God's family as a two-part decision: "Yet to all who received him [Jesus], to those who believed in his name, he gave the right to become children of God." You must receive Christ and believe in his name. Even though the Bible teaches that Jesus created the universe (John 1:3), he never forces anyone to follow him. The choice is yours! By "receiving" Jesus, you accept that he was God, the perfect picture of what God is like. By "believing in his name," you are saying that you know Jesus paid the price for your sin when he died on the cross. John 3:16 says, "For God so loved the world that he gave his one and only Son, that whoever believes in him shall not perish but have eternal life." God came to earth because he loves every one of us and wants us to have eternal life with him. Jesus describes eternal life in John 17:3, "Now this is eternal life: that they may know you, the only true God, and Jesus Christ, whom you have sent." Eternal life is knowing Jesus. If you aren't sure whether or not you have done that, take a minute right now and make sure. If you aren't used to praying or if you don't know what to pray, **here's a prayer that you can pray...**

getting started

God, I want to become a follower of Jesus. I receive Jesus into my life. I believe he is God and that he came to pay the price for my sin when he died on the cross. Please forgive me for living life my own way. I turn away from that life and turn toward you. As best I know how and with your grace and strength, I want to live for you from this day forward. Amen.

Now that you have surrendered your life to Jesus and believed what he came to do, you can be certain that you are part of God's family!

There are a few things that are important to keep in mind right from the beginning...

First, becoming a follower of Jesus is not just about learning stuff. It's much more than that. Jesus said that those who come to him, hear his words, and put them into practice will be the ones who will have a foundation to stand on when tough times come. Building a solid foundation means that you bring everything to Christ, hear God's Word (the Bible), and then put it into practice (do something about it).

Second, most of us learn best from watching and learning from others. That's why we encourage you to put yourself in these four places: (1) a large gathering where you can worship God and hear teaching from the Bible (a youth group and/or a church service), (2) a small group where you can apply the Bible to your life and live out your faith with friends, (3) a one-on-one mentoring meeting with a spiritual coach, and (4) a private time with God on your own. *Learning to Follow Jesus: Youth Edition* is a tool that can help you develop in your private time with God and can serve as a conversation starter with you and your coach. We all need people who we can share our honest thoughts, our successes, our failures, and our questions with, especially when we are just starting out on something new. A spiritual coach and the people in your small group will help you learn how to honor God in every area of life. They probably won't have all the answers to your questions, but they are committed to sharing what they do know with you.

What church and/or youth group do you plan to attend?..

If you don't have a spiritual coach or a small group yet, please contact a youth pastor/leader to get more information and to help you find both.

Third, following Christ is a process. You will not be perfect, neither will your spiritual coach or the people in your small group! Only Jesus is perfect. When you follow Christ, you accept what he has done for you. **Knowing that your eternal destiny depends on Jesus' righteousness and not yours will set you free from trying to work to get God to love you.** Jesus has already pleased

God for you! There's nothing you can ever do to make God love you more. You are loved! His love for you is limitless and eternal. His thoughts about you are always good. Enjoy knowing that God is pleased with you because of Jesus. Don't try to work to make him happy. Just live your life thankful for his amazing love and acceptance. As you spend time with other followers of Christ and with your loving Heavenly Father, you will realize that you want to become more like Christ, and you will change. God will change you.

***Before coaching, please review the "What Is a Spiritual Coach?" Resource on page 276**

Introduce yourself if you don't know the person.

Turn to the "Getting Started" page and emphasize the following:

- Congratulate him or her! Choosing to intentionally follow Jesus is the most important decision of this person's life.
- Explain the importance of coming to Christ, hearing his words, and putting them into practice.
- Explain the importance of getting involved in a small group.
- Explain that you are his or her spiritual coach. Let them know that it will be fine with you if, for any reason, he or she would rather have a different coach. You will not be offended. Getting a coach with whom you have good chemistry is important. It is also important that spiritual coaches be the same gender as those they are coaching.
- Talk about the importance of setting aside about fifteen minutes a day for time with God. Ask when that will work best. (See the fill in for this.) Have him or her write it in the book.
- Encourage them to write in their book. It will help them apply more to their life.
- Make sure the person has a Bible in a modern translation (NIV, NLT). Make them aware of www.youversion.com where they can find the Bible in a preferred translation and free reading plans. If

applicable, they can also search "YouVersion®" in the app store and find the Bible (provided by LifeChurch.tv) for free there as well.

- Show them how to do the Scripture memory and make use of the fill-in-the-blank areas.
- Encourage them to pray before they start.
- Remind them that the key is reviewing daily.
- Tell them you will have them recite the verse when you get together.

Review the Seven Qualities from the Table of Contents.

- Show them how each of the seven qualities has a chapter and steps all its own.
- Encourage them to read one step a day, letting them know you will cover one quality each time you meet over the next seven weeks.

Ask him or her if they have any questions.

Ask how you can pray for them. You may want to write this down and pray for them during the week.

Pray that God will bless this teenager as he or she takes the next steps as a follower of Christ.

Exchange phone numbers and e-mail addresses.

Set a time for the next meeting(s).

Note: It is best to get a weekly time of about an hour that works for both of you. Try to schedule out for one or two months if possible.

Review "Using This Book" and explain the icons to them.

This book is designed to help you develop good habits that will support your journey with Christ. To get the most out of this, you will need to make the following choices:

- Spend fifteen minutes a day to focus on your spiritual growth. Every relationship takes time. Your relationship with Christ is no different. Choose a time slot that you can always do. Whether it's in the morning, at night, or both, the important thing is that you make time for your spiritual growth. You may have to try a couple of different times but pick a time that works for you.

What time will work best for you every day?..

- Write your answers in this book. You'll remember more of what you are learning if you take the time to write your answers. Be sure to answer them before your scheduled discussion with your spiritual coach. Like the question you've answered above, all the questions for you to answer will be outlined by a gray box.
- Commit to meeting with a spiritual coach once a week over the next seven weeks, covering one quality per week. This is the recommended timeline; however, there may be a different one that you and your spiritual coach can agree on.
- Read the Bible references for yourself. If you don't have a Bible in a modern translation (New

International Version [NIV] and New Living Translation [NLT] are good ones), ask your spiritual coach to help you find one.

- Memorize the Scripture. The verse will be listed at the beginning of each quality. Do your best to learn it word-for-word. It will be much easier than you think! Go over the verse every day; that puts it into your long-term memory. You won't regret it!
- Put what you learn into practice right away. A follower of Jesus is someone who learns what Jesus is like and then takes action to become like him.

Before you get started, there are some symbols that you should understand:

When you see this symbol, it's an opportunity to pray. Feel free to also use your own words, but these will help you get started.

Following this symbol there will be thoughts and questions for your spiritual coach to discuss with you.

When you see this symbol, you will know there are valuable resources to help you dig a little deeper.

When you see this symbol, it will be followed by an action step for you to take. Respond to it right away!

Enjoy the journey!

QUALITY 1

LEARN TO BE WITH JESUS

learn to BE WITH JESUS

The more time you spend with Jesus, the more you will love him and become like him. That's why it is so important to learn how to be with him.

As a follower of Jesus, you are learning how to make Jesus the leader of your life. Before you may have just done things without thinking much of him, but now that you know he is always with you, you might start to see things or do things differently. You are letting him show you life from his perspective. In this quality we are going to focus on learning how to enjoy being with him every day regardless of what else is going on.

The best time to be with him is during a "quiet time." A quiet devotional time is a good start, but Jesus is *always* with you. As you learn "to remain in him," to be with him, he will change everything! He'll show you how to live life to the fullest while bringing him honor. He'll teach you through his Word (the Bible) and during your prayer time how to hear his voice. He'll even show you how to love people and to live a joyful life. Sound good? It is! Serving Jesus is the best life! That's what this quality is all about.

learn to REMAIN IN HIM

"Come to me, all you who are weary and burdened, and I will give you rest. Take my yoke upon you and learn from me, for I am gentle and humble in heart, and you will find rest for your souls. For my yoke is easy and my burden is light." Matthew 11:28–30

Read: John 15:1–10

I (Claude) am a pretty independent guy. I had always found a kind of comfort in the thought that I didn't need anyone. In fact, I had come to the conclusion that needing others was a sign of weakness. As a result, I had been known to take on more than I should. This was clearly a pride issue. My desire to do things on my own strength was a form of idolatry. Instead of turning to Christ, I was turning to myself! The reality is that anything of any worth in my life is a result of Jesus' redemptive work. I fall short every time and my "loner" mentality left me only feeling alone. It took me realizing that Christ was truly alone on the cross so that I would never have to be alone as a follower of Christ to finally surrender!

As you read John 15, did you notice how important it is that we remain in Christ, staying connected to him and dependent on him as our starting place for life? God has a purpose for each one of our lives. Jesus uses an analogy of a vine and the fruit it produces to make this point. His purpose is that we would "bear fruit" in his world. We are not on this planet for ourselves or to find *our* purpose. We are here for him and to fulfill *his* purpose.

Who does Jesus say is the vine?..

What is the role of the Father?..

What is the role of the follower of Christ?..

The word "remain" appears eleven times in John 15:1–10, always meaning to stay close and connected to Jesus. I'll remind us again…following Jesus is always about staying close to and remaining in him.

What promise does Jesus give us in the first part of John 15:4?..

....

If you remain in him, he promises to remain in you. Do you want to remain in Christ? There's a great passage in James 4:8 that says something similar: "Come near to God and he will come near to you."

God has been reaching out to you, desiring to rescue you. You have to decide to reach out to him.

Reaching out to God by deciding to remain in him is a form of worship. To "worship" God simply means you choose to serve him with your whole life. You declare to God that he is the leader of your life and that you want to honor him with your whole life. Some people sing to God as a form of worship. We also express our love, thankfulness, and commitment to God at our youth group or church services. I encourage you to start to do this right away. There is something powerful that happens when you reach out to God. It's important to know that you can also do this at home or anywhere. Worship should be a lifestyle. You may want to check out the list of suggested songs for each of the qualities on the website (www.learningtofollow.net). These songs are available to you on your journey. If you would like some help with this, talk with your spiritual coach about it. He or she should be able to help you.

Based on John 15:1–4, why can't we do this on our own?..

....

We are going to talk more about some of the ways we can learn to remain in him over the upcoming days. Right now you may realize, as I do, that you need to repent for trying to live life on your own without God. Let's take a few minutes right now to just enjoy that we are connected to Christ.

Dear Jesus, thank you for the invitation to follow you. It is amazing to me that you want me to remain close to you forever. I am humbled that you, the Creator of the universe, would love me and desire to be close to me and me to you. You are the final authority in my life and I want to honor you with my life. Forgive me for trying to do life on my own. I turn away from trying to do life my own way and I turn to you. I accept your invitation to remain in you and your promise to remain in me. I realize that I can't bear the kind of fruit that you have planned for my life on my own. I live for you. Amen.

Write out the following words "I am in you" on an index card. Look at the card during the day and let your awareness of God's presence in you affect how you live your life.

....

....

....

....

NOTES

learn to RECOGNIZE FRUIT

"Come to___, all you who are______and burdened, and I will give you____. Take my_____upon you and learn from___, for I am gentle and_______in heart, and you will find rest for your____. For my_____is easy and my burden is____." ______ 11:28–30

◁ MEMORIZE SCRIPTURE

"Come to me, all you who are weary and burdened, and I will give you rest. Take my yoke upon you and learn from me, for I am gentle and humble in heart, and you will find rest for your souls. For my yoke is easy and my burden is light." Matthew 11:28–30

Read: John 15:5–6; Galatians 5:22–23

I (Claude) love fruit. Some of my favorite childhood memories involve picking fresh strawberries, cherries, and raspberries. There is nothing like eating freshly picked fruit! You haven't enjoyed the fall until you've picked an apple off the tree and taken a bite. I can almost hear the snap! Good fruit...

Who does Jesus say is the vine and what are we?..

Why do you think Jesus wants us to stay connected with the Father?..

....

Jesus says in John 15:5, "If a man remains in me and I in him, he will bear much fruit." In other words, if you stay close to God, the fruit of your life will reflect God. The reality is, you can't bear godly fruit on your own. I will put it another way. If you go to an apple tree, what do you expect? If you go to a grape vine, what do you expect? The same is true with God. If you stay connected to God, what can you expect? God lets us know what his fruit is like in Galatians 5:22–23.

The fruit of the Spirit is:

- **Love** ▹ loving people without expecting anything back, no strings attached
- **Joy** ▹ delight, being filled with happiness because God is amazingly good and satisfying
- **Peace** ▹ health and wholeness in relationships and personal well being
- **Patience** ▹ extended restraint of anger and anxiety
- **Kindness** ▹ friendly, regardless of how people treat you
- **Goodness** ▹ being generous and caring to people
- **Faithfulness** ▹ confident trust in God that results in reliable actions
- **Gentleness** ▹ humility, considerateness, meekness, preferring others
- **Self-control** ▹ disciplined, control over actions and appetites

The fruit (which is ALL of the above) should be noticeable in the life of a follower of Jesus!

Which of these is lacking the most in your life right now?...

What would change if that fruit were more evident in your life?...

....

Make whatever you mentioned above a matter of prayer. Ask God to make his fruit evident in your life. When you remain in Christ, you and others will begin to see God's fruit in your life. Isn't he awesome? Like any fruit, it takes time to grow. Don't become impatient with yourself when it doesn't happen overnight. Just stay close to Jesus, delighting in him and in his Word. Trust him. When you notice some fruit, thank him for it. Enjoy the changes he is bringing about in your life.

The end of John 15:5 reminds us that becoming like Christ is not something we do on our own or by our own efforts. Notice that it says clearly, "Apart from me you can do nothing." Wow! So much for trying to produce godly fruit on your own! Can't do it! Don't even try it without the Lord.

Lord, thank you for confirming that you are my source and that you will produce fruit in my life as I remain in you. I look forward to it. I pray that nothing in my life will inhibit your fruit from growing in me. I don't want to grow fruit so that people will look at me. I want to grow it so that people will look to you and so that you will receive the glory. Change me to be more like you! Amen.

learn to BE WITH HIM AS YOU READ SCRIPTURE

"Come to___, all____who are________ ____ ________, and I will_____ _____ _____.
Take my______ ______ _____and learn______ _____, for I am______ _____ ______ ___
____, and you will______ ______ ______ _____ _____. For my_____ ____ ______and my
______ _____." ________ __:28–30

"Come to me, all you who are weary and burdened, and I will give you rest. Take my yoke upon you and learn from me, for I am gentle and humble in heart, and you will find rest for your souls. For my yoke is easy and my burden is light." Matthew 11:28–30

Read: John 15:7; John 1:1–18; Psalm 1

Notice John 15:7, "If you remain in me and my words remain in you..." Part of remaining in him is that his words need to remain in us. Earlier in this Gospel, in John 1:1–4, Jesus is described this way:

> *In the beginning was the Word, and the Word was with God, and the Word was God. He was with God in the beginning. Through him all things were made; without him nothing was made that has been made. In him was life, and that life was the light of men.*

Then, John 1:14a states, "The Word became flesh and made his dwelling among us." The point is this: Jesus is the exact representation of what God is like. When you want to know what God is like, look at Jesus.

In order to really look at Jesus, you are going to have to read and review the four books of the Bible that tell you specifically about him (Matthew, Mark, Luke, and John). In these books, you learn how he thinks and acts in various situations.

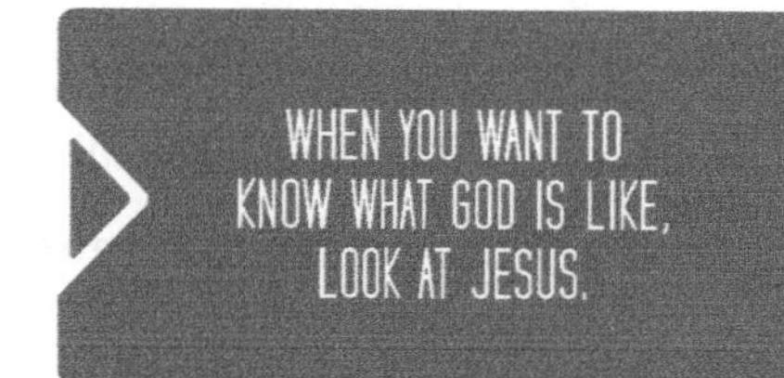
WHEN YOU WANT TO
KNOW WHAT GOD IS LIKE,
LOOK AT JESUS.

The rest of the New Testament (Acts through Revelation) tells you how Jesus continued and continues to lead and direct his followers (the church) since his death and resurrection. But it doesn't stop there. Jesus also said that the rest of the Bible points to him: "Everything must be fulfilled that is written about me in the Law of Moses, the Prophets and the Psalms" (Luke 24:44). As a follower of Jesus, you will want to eventually read and study the entire Bible so you can allow his words to remain in you.

The idea of reading and studying the whole Bible may seem like a huge deal right now. Don't let it overwhelm you. Just read a little bit each day and apply it to your life. As you start to develop your quiet time with God, I recommend you do the following:

- Set a regular time and a place. It should be a quiet and a private place. Remember Jesus' words in Matthew 6:6: "But when you pray, go into your room, close the door and pray to your Father, who is unseen. Then your Father, who sees what is done in secret, will reward you." I like the morning because it helps me start the day off right. Some prefer the evening. The important thing is that you make regular time for God. What time and place works best for you?

- Decide on a Bible reading plan.
  - Read straight through an entire book of the Bible, one at a time, at your own pace. I encourage you to start with the Gospel of Matthew since that is the primary book we are studying.
  - Don't read so much that you can't spend time really thinking about its meaning. Many people start with a chapter a day.[1]
  - Don't jump around as you read, reading a few verses here and there in one book or another. You will be better able to understand what you are reading if you read it in context (the order in which it was intended to be read).
- Pray for guidance before you start reading. Ask the Holy Spirit to guide you into truth through his Word. Remember, he is with you.
- Make notes of what you notice and what you think God may be speaking to you as you read. I (Claude) use the YouVersion® Bible on my iPad and make notes by clicking on the "notes" tab. I also highlight Scripture on this app. You can access this Bible tool via the website www.youversion.com as well. Whether you use that tool or an actual physical Bible, the point is for you to make note of what the Word of God is showing you so you can reflect on those moments.
- Prayerfully respond to what you are reading. If you notice something in your life needs to change, pray that God will help you change it. If you notice an aspect of God that is encouraging, thank God for it. If an action is needed, ask God for wisdom in how to carry out the action.
- Remember your focus is on Jesus and not the habit of having a quiet time.

Jesus, thank you for providing a way for me to remain in you through your Word. Open my mind to your thoughts, ways, and ideas. Teach me how to remain in your words so you can bear your fruit through me. Help me to set aside a specific time each day at............................to meet with you and to read your Word. I rest in your guidance. Amen.

NOTES

learn to BE WITH CHRIST IN PRAYER

"Come ___ ___, all ___ ___ ___ ___ ___ ___ ___, and I ___ ___ ___ ___. Take ___ ___ ___ ___ ___ ___ ___ ___ ___, for ___ ___ ___ ___ ___ ___ ___, and you ___ ___ ___ ___ ___ ___. For ___ ___ ___ ___ ___ ___ ___ ___ ___." ___ ___ ___:___-___

"Come to me, all you who are weary and burdened, and I will give you rest. Take my yoke upon you and learn from me, for I am gentle and humble in heart, and you will find rest for your souls. For my yoke is easy and my burden is light." Matthew 11:28–30

Read: John 15:7; Matthew 7:7–12; James 4:2–3

In the previous step, we focused on the first half of John 15:7 that reminded us of the importance of remaining connected with God. In this step, we are focusing on the effect this has on our prayer life: "If you remain in me and my words remain in you, ask whatever you wish, and it will be given you." When you remain in Jesus and remain in his Word, you will learn to pray his kind of prayers, and God will answer them. Prayer is not about saying the right words and "presto," getting your wish.

The Lord does not give you everything you want or even everything you ask for.

What does James 4:2–3 say are the reasons why some prayers are not answered?........................

....

The invitation is to get close to Jesus so you know the things about which he cares most. When you align your heart with his desires, there is no end to what can happen in prayer. God values your creativity. He says that if you remain in him and in his Word, then you can ask him for what is in your heart. Prayer is less about asking for what you want and is more about praying in line with God's perfect will for your life. There is a whole world of discovery between you and God. Stay close to him and start asking him for great things for his kingdom. He just might say, "Great idea!" and make it happen.

It is important to know that God answers your prayers. We simply don't like that sometimes the answer is "no" or "not yet." But he is always good and has a perspective that we don't. We can find joy in knowing that he hears us, and answers with our best interest in mind. I would hate the idea that I don't have something because I simply didn't ask!

In Matthew 7:7–11, Jesus says something similar:

> *Ask and it will be given to you; seek and you will find; knock and the door will be opened to you. For everyone who asks receives; he who seeks finds; and to him who knocks, the door will be opened. Which of you, if his son asks for bread, will give him a stone? Or if he asks*

> *for a fish, will give him a snake? If you, then, though you are evil, know how to give good gifts to your children, how much more will your Father in heaven give good gifts to those who ask him!*

In short, stay close to the Lord to learn his heart. Pray Jesus' kind of prayers and you can count on your Heavenly Father to answer them.

I have talked with some people who think they should pray only when they absolutely have to, as if you only get so many answered prayers in your life so you had better save them for when you really need them. That isn't how God is! He tells us to ask. That's not my idea. Those are his words. Ask! Just ask!

Why not talk with God right now? Got anything on your mind you would like him to answer? Talk with him about it! I have modeled some of my prayers up to this point. It's time for you to fly solo a little bit. I'll help you with suggestions.

1. Talk with God like you would a good friend.
2. Thank God for what he is doing in your life right now.
3. If something about this lesson stood out to you, talk with him about it.
4. Ask God in your own words for the things that are on your mind and then tell him that you will trust him.

learn how REMAINING IN CHRIST AFFECTS OTHERS

MEMORIZE SCRIPTURE ◁

"_______ ___ _____, ____ _____ _____ _____ ________ _____ __________, _____ __ _____ ______ _____ ______.

____ ____ ______ _______ _____ _____ ______ _____ _____, _____ __ ___ _______ _____ _______ __

______, _____ _____ _____ ______ ______ _____ ______ ______. _____ _____ ______ __ ______ _____ _____

_________ ___ _____." _________ ___:___-___

"Come to me, all you who are weary and burdened, and I will give you rest. Take my yoke upon you and learn from me, for I am gentle and humble in heart, and you will find rest for your souls. For my yoke is easy and my burden is light." Matthew 11:28–30

Read: John 15:9–12

Unfortunately, the truth is, there are some people who claim to be followers of Christ who are simply awful to be around. They are flat-out negative. They seem to have the attitude that following Jesus is a burden they have to carry. They have made a decision to get through it, kind of like you get through a dentist appointment! I don't know what Bible they are reading, but that's not what Jesus had in mind for his followers, as this passage clearly shows.

First, Jesus reminds us of how much he loves us, "As the Father has loved me, so have I loved You." We see glimpses of the Father's love for his Son, Jesus, throughout the Scriptures. At Jesus' baptism, the Father confirms his love for the Son. He says, "This is my Son, whom I love; with him I am well pleased" (Matthew 3:17). Then, when Jesus was on a mountain with several of his disciples, the Father again declares his love, "This is my Son, whom I love; with him I am well pleased. Listen to him!" (Matthew 17:5). In Jesus' prayer right before he died, several times he mentions God's amazing love for him, "I have made you known to them, and will continue to make you known in order that the love you have for me may be in them and that I myself may be in them" (John 17:26). Jesus said simply that the love he received from the Father, he has given to us. He just calls us to remain in that love. Then, Jesus tells us how to remain in his love.

How do we remain in his love according to verse 10?...

....

According to verse 12, what is his command?...

This is the part that my friends who are not following Jesus don't get. It's not a huge burden to give away something so wonderful as the love of Jesus.

Did someone ever give you a special gift? Maybe it was tickets to a special athletic event, or a friend inviting you to join his or her family on a great vacation that you couldn't afford. Maybe someone gave his time to just listen when you needed it the most. I (Daniel) can think of lots of these, but one stands out to me right now. I was going through a difficult struggle just after we moved to Texas when I was in high school. I had a sister who was twelve years older than I who lived in Wisconsin at that time with her husband. Because she knew me and wanted me to know I was loved, she used to send me packages with articles about Christian athletes and a whole bunch of other meaningful things. At the time, I was too "cool" to let her know how much those expressions of love meant to me, but I looked for them in the mail. I read every article she sent. It was a lifeline to a fifteen-year-old who needed to know he was loved. Then, to top it off, she would call me, or my parents would let me call her sometimes, and she would take the time with me to talk about what was on my mind. It really helped me get through a tough time. Here's my point: after I got through that time, I thought about how caring my sister was, and it made me want to be like that for others. I want to do for others what I experienced. It's not a big burden, because I know what being cared for feels like.

Take a minute to write down some thoughts (just a few words or phrases) that you can later discuss with your coach about a time when you felt loved, cared for, etc., and were inspired to do something similar for another person.

....

....

That's all Jesus is saying in this passage. Just give away the love you are experiencing from him. It's not a burden. In fact, it is just the opposite. It's fun. It brings you joy. Jesus says in verse 11, "I have told you this so that my joy may be in you and that your joy may be complete." His command is just that we would love others like he has loved us. Remaining in Christ's love will cause you to want to show his love to others. The more you receive from him, the more you are going to want to share it with others!

Sometimes my heart goes out to "Christians" who are not having fun following Jesus. I wonder if they have ever stayed in Christ's presence long enough to experience his amazing love. Decide now that you won't miss out on it. You now know the secret of the joyful Christian life. Stay close to Jesus and give away what he gives to you. He will change the world around you if you will do that.

Continue to draw me close to you, Jesus. Thank you for your amazing love and friendship. Help me to give away to others what you have given to me so the world will know you are real and that you love them.

NOTES

QUALITY 1
RESOURCES

How to Develop a Schedule

1. **Values**
   The values of a follower of Jesus are two-fold: loving God and loving people.
2. **Roles**
   God has given you specific roles (son, brother, friend, student, athlete, etc.) and resources to manage (time, talent, energy, and money). Identify your roles and resources.
3. **Tasks**
   Make a list of tasks you perform under each role you fill.
4. **Time**
   Estimate the amount of time each task will take on a weekly basis so that Christ is honored. Add up the hours and subtract from 168. Although you should include time to sleep (at least 8–9 hours per night is recommended), not every minute should be scheduled. In fact, about 5–10 hours of your week should not be scheduled.
5. **Review**
   Set aside time weekly to evaluate and plan how you will spend your time based on your values.
6. **Record** the hours on a weekly schedule.

In addition to notes, you can use the area on the following pages to begin creating a schedule...

QUALITY 1 ▹ DECISIONS, NOTES, PRAYERS...

COACH'S SECTION

Relate

Tell me a little bit about your family (parents, brothers, sisters).

As we start this journey together, it might be helpful for you to know a little bit about my faith journey.

Note: Share your faith journey.

Important: It's very important that they hear how Jesus changed your life. This should be a 5–10 minute testimony maximum.

Tell me about your faith journey. How did you decide to make a commitment to Christ?

Note: Be a good listener. Express appropriate emotion but don't side track conversation. Summarize what you hear them saying. Be sensitive to the leading of the Holy Spirit. Don't push if they decide to say things vaguely.

Review

Were you able to find a small group that worked for you? (Skip this question if your youth ministry doesn't currently have small groups available).

How did it go with your 5–15 minutes each day with the Lord?

Let's see how far you can get in reciting Matthew 11:28–30…

If the student went through First Steps: Youth Edition: Do you still remember Matthew 4:19?

Reflect

What stood out to you this week in your reading of Quality One?

Step 1 – Did you download any worship songs from iTunes? Would you like song recommendations?

Step 3 – Did you download the "YouVersion®" app or visit the website? How's your Bible reading going?

If it is in line with the discussion, feel free to ask for them to share any answers to questions that they may have recorded in their book this week.

Refocus

What decisions did you make as a result of what stood out to you?

Resource

How would you like support in the decisions you made this week?

Note: See the "How to Develop a Schedule" resource on page 47 if help is needed on the schedule.

Review

Did anything confuse you this week as you read?

Prayer

How can I pray for you this week?

Note: Turn to the prayer list you started for this person.

Ask if God has answered their requests from the previous week.

Take them by the hand (for young men the handshake posture is not threatening).

Pray for what they asked and that God would bless them in their next steps as a follower of Christ.

Set the date and time for the next meeting, schedule out for 1–2 months if possible.

QUALITY 2

LEARN TO LISTEN

learn to LISTEN

It's important to realize that the first thing Jesus did after calling his disciples to follow him was to invite them to listen and watch as he taught in the synagogues and healed people (Matthew 4:23–25). Most people would expect him to take some time to build a relationship and to teach his disciples privately. Not Jesus! He took them right into the middle of real ministry where they could hear his words and see them put into practice right away.

As you are learning to listen to Jesus, it's important to know he will speak to you in four ways: through his written Word (the Bible); through prayer; in real life situations; and through his people, the church.

Still, hearing Jesus' words is not enough. You need to *do* what he says. Matthew 7:24–25 records Jesus words:

> Therefore everyone who *hears* these words of mine and *puts them into practice* is like a wise man who built his house on the rock. The rain came down, the streams rose, and the winds blew and beat against that house; yet it did not fall, because it had its foundation on the rock. [Emphasis mine.]

As a follower of Jesus, you will want to be in places where you can hear the teachings of Jesus and see him change lives. Acts 2:46 describes the earliest followers of Jesus meeting regularly in large gatherings (the temple courts) and in small groups (homes). We need both. That's why we have both large groups (worship services) and the small groups (however they may look in your youth ministry). At both our Sunday morning and youth service, we worship God, hear his Word taught, and serve others. It's also a great place to bring a friend who wants to see what following Christ is all about. In our small groups, we ask questions, encourage one another, and learn how to hear and apply God's Word to our daily lives. We also have Jesus' assurance that he is with us in a real way, "For where two or three come together in my name, there am I with them" (Matthew 18:20). In both size groups, however, it is really important to focus on learning to hear the words of Jesus so you can put them into practice.

Besides a large service and a small group, it is also important to learn to hear Jesus by reading the Bible. One of the problems that I (Claude) faced while learning to follow Jesus was thinking *attending* meant *knowing*. I thought that because I attended church, listened to the preacher and prayed before bed and meals that I knew Jesus. I even asked him to be the leader of my life (several times, trying to make sure I'd go to heaven) but still tried to do good things under my own strength. I knew about God most of my life but didn't really know him until I decided to simply follow him.

In this quality we are going to focus on learning to carefully hear the words of Jesus in the Scriptures so you can put them into practice. Besides attending a corporate worship service and a small group, I am encouraging you to set aside at least fifteen minutes each day for "hearing" time. **As you learn to hear the Word of God, you need to develop the habit of "doing" it right away**. There shouldn't be a lot of time between "hearing" and "doing." Jesus expects you to act on what you know. Don't make the mistake of assuming that this means the expectation is for you to have a list of things "to do." This is a time to hear what has been "done" so you can learn what being with him looks like. You don't need to learn a lot each day, just enough so you can apply it to your life that day.

We'll talk more about this throughout this quality, but first I would like to give you some advice:

- Choose a Bible reading plan that works for you. I suggest reading the passages in this guide as your reading for now. You may want to read the entire book of Matthew when you are done. After that you might want to work your way through the New Testament. The important thing is that you make Bible reading a normal part of your day (www.youversion.com is a great place to find reading plans).
- Pray before you start reading. Ask God to point out things to you. Don't rush through your Bible reading. Read with an open mind and heart.
- When something stands out to you, underline it in your Bible. It is easy to go back and review if it is marked in some way.
- Write down what stood out to you. I highlight passages in the YouVersion® Bible app on my iPad or iPhone. I am also able to make notes attached to whatever verse I highlight so I can look back at what God has laid on my heart. A lot of times a specific verse will stand out to me. When that happens, I'll write the verse on an index card and think or write through how that verse effects my life that day.
- Pray. Ask God how he wants you to act on what stood out to you that day. Some days you will

have something significant to apply. At other times, you will have something to think about. The important thing is that you read and apply it right away.

You might want to talk with your coach about how your devotional time is going. Don't give up on the process if you are struggling with setting time aside regularly. Developing a new habit takes time and effort. Most people say it takes twenty-one days to make a new habit. Stay with it. Just do it. I believe you will find God's Word to have a powerful influence on your life if you will develop the habit of learning to listen.

When will you do your Bible reading and "listening" time?...

Are you involved in a small group? If so, what does it look like and how is it going?.........................

....

Lord, help me to learn to listen to your words so I can apply them to the life you have given me. Build a foundation that will last when the tough times in life come. Be the center of my life from this day forward. Help me to faithfully apply your Word to my life. Give me the strength to be a doer of your Word and not just a hearer. I ask this in Jesus' name, amen.

learn to BE HAPPY

"Therefore everyone who hears these words of mine and puts them into practice is like a wise man who built his house on the rock. The rain came down, the streams rose, and the winds blew and beat against that house; yet it did not fall, because it had its foundation on the rock." Matthew 7:24–25

Scripture Memory Review: Matthew 11:28–30

Read: Matthew 5:1–12

What words are repeated in Matthew 5:1–12?..

Each of the nine statements in this section begins with Jesus saying, "Blessed." Some translators actually translate the word *blessed* as "happy." This is not a bad translation, but the English word *happy* is too shallow for what the word means. I'll do my best to explain what *blessed* means.

> In secular Greece the island of Cyprus was called the blest island. The idea was that those who lived in Cyprus never had to leave its shores in order to have all they needed to be content...the island was self-contained. No one had to search for the needs and wants of life.[1]

That's partly what *blessed* means—when you have it, you are fortunate and satisfied and you don't have to look anywhere else for it.

The Old Testament meaning of *blessed* meant you were approved by God. In other words, you can't be a blessed person and not be approved by God. "When we are blessed by God, our happiness does not come from circumstances, or by accident, or through a diligent search. It comes because we stand approved before the Creator of the universe."[2]

According to these verses, who is blessed?..

....

What surprises you about those who are blessed?..

....

In these verses, Jesus teaches us the truth, something we would never discover on our own. He teaches that blessing is not linked to how much you have in this world. Blessed people are those who realize they have nothing to bring to God, the poor in spirit. If you discover that truth, regardless of how much money you have, you literally will receive it all—the kingdom of heaven, the mother lode of all gifts. Blessing is for everyone who knows the truth about what he or she has before God. We have nothing to offer him except our lives and he has everything to offer us. These verses illustrate how important it is to come to Christ to learn from him what life, blessing, and everything else in life is all about.

What kinds of things do you tend to rely on to find your sense of worth and value?..........................

....

How would your life be different if you found all of your significance and value in God?..................

....

....

With these verses Jesus offers blessing and hope for every person on the planet. For those who are mourning, he promises comfort. For those who prefer others ahead of themselves (the meek), he promises a huge inheritance. For those who are hungry and thirsty to do right things (righteousness), he promises they will be satisfied. For those who are merciful, he promises mercy. For those who are pure in heart, he promises an audience with God. For those who seek peace, he promises to call them his family. For those who are persecuted in this life, he promises that God's kingdom belongs to them. They get it all. For those who are insulted and spoken against, Jesus says they can rejoice because they are in great company; that's what happened to the prophets and eventually to Jesus. You simply can't lose when you find everything in God.

Take a few moments to think about how you have nothing except your life to offer God. Take a moment right now to close your eyes and turn your open palms upward as a symbol of your poverty of spirit. Now talk with God about that.

Heavenly Father, I realize I have nothing to offer you except my life. Although it's broken and messed up, it's all I have. I give my life back to you. I realize I am poor in spirit but you say that I am blessed because of that. That's very encouraging to me. It gives me hope. I come to you the same as every other person under your leadership comes: empty-handed. You give me everything. I receive your kingdom in my life. You are so good. Have your way in my life.

NOTES

learn to GO TO THE SOURCE

"Therefore__________who hears these________of mine and puts them into ________is like a______man who built his________on the rock. The______came down, the streams_____, and the winds blew and_____against that house; yet it did not___, because it had its___________on the rock." ________7:24–25

"Therefore everyone who hears these words of mine and puts them into practice is like a wise man who built his house on the rock. The rain came down, the streams rose, and the winds blew and beat against that house; yet it did not fall, because it had its foundation on the rock." Matthew 7:24–25

Read: 2 Timothy 3:16–17

Reading Scripture will be an important part of your growth as a follower of Christ. 2 Timothy 3:16–17 describes what makes Scripture so important and the huge role it will have in your life as a follower.

What claim does 2 Timothy 3:16 make?..

"God-breathed" means "inspired by God." It means that God communicated his message through the thoughts and vocabulary of the human writers. It doesn't mean he "dictated" it, but it does mean that God directed the writer even in the selection of his words so that God's intent and purpose come through. It's amazing to realize that God has given us, in writing, his thoughts in human language. Pretty cool.

In what four ways does this passage say that Scripture can help you? Write them below.

....

....

If you wrote teaching, rebuking, correcting and training in righteousness, you are correct. Scripture will help you learn information about God and how to follow Christ (teaching). It will help you discover things you are doing that you need to surrender to Christ (rebuking). It will help you realize how Christ can restore you and reestablish your foundation so you can be who you were designed to be (correcting). And, it will help train and discipline you to honor God with your life and actions (training in righteousness). Isn't it great that you can know where to find the answers to those life questions?

How's your plan to have regular Bible reading in your life going? What are some of the struggles you're having?..

Below you'll find some questions for you to answer and later discuss with your spiritual coach. (He or she may or may not know the answers, but can get answers from one of the leaders of the church.) Take some time to really consider them and then write down your thoughts in the space provided.

What specific questions do you have about God?

What questions do you have about what it means to be a follower of Jesus?

....

....

....

....

....

....

Are there things you are doing in your life that you are aware need to be surrendered to God so he can change you now that you're a follower of Jesus? If so, what are they?..

....

What areas of your life do you feel need to be made new again so you can build a solid foundation with God?..

God is in the process of changing your life and mine. He loves you with a never-ending love. There is nothing you can do to make God love you more or make him love you less. In fact, God loves you so much that he doesn't want you to settle for a ripped-off version of your life. He wants you to become all that he has designed you to become. For that to happen, he needs to change you. There is your work and there is his work. Your work is to ask God and to submit yourself to him. It is God's will to change you into his likeness. That will happen as you regularly put yourself in a situation to hear God's Word and to put it into practice. Call to mind again Jesus' words in Matthew 7:24–25:

> *Therefore everyone who hears these words of mine and puts them into practice is like a wise man who built his house on the rock. The rain came down, the streams rose, and the winds blew and beat against that house; yet it did not fall, because it had its foundation on the rock.*

What decision(s) are you making today?..

....

....

Heavenly Father, thank you for your Word that guides me into truth. Help me to make the Scriptures part of my everyday life. With your help, I am going to attempt to read the Bible each day. I need to know your thoughts so I can know how to please you and live the life you have designed me to live. I ask for your help with this. I want to please you. Amen.

learn to SEE JESUS IN SCRIPTURE

"Therefore________who______these______of mine and_____them into
______is like a_____man who_____his______on the____. The_____ _____
down, the streams____, and the_____ _____and____against that house; yet
it___ ___ ____, because it had its_________on the____." ________:24–25

"Therefore everyone who hears these words of mine and puts them into practice is like a wise man who built his house on the rock. The rain came down, the streams rose, and the winds blew and beat against that house; yet it did not fall, because it had its foundation on the rock." Matthew 7:24–25

Read: Luke 24:13–49

What stands out to you about these accounts?..

....

....

After Jesus' resurrection from the dead he appeared to his disciples. Jesus said something very interesting in Luke 24:44, "Everything must be fulfilled that is written about me in the Law of Moses, the Prophets and the Psalms." Verse 45 says, "Then he opened their minds so they could understand the Scriptures." At least two things are important about this. First, Jesus pointed his followers to read the Scriptures to understand who he was. Second, Jesus helped them understand by opening their minds. Both are true for you and other followers of Jesus.

It might be helpful to learn some basic things about the Bible. Open your Bible to the front cover and turn each page until you find what looks like a table of contents. You will notice that the Bible is made up of two parts: the Old Testament and the New Testament. The Old Testament was written down and took place before Jesus' earthly life. The New Testament was written by his followers after Jesus' resurrection.

The Old Testament is made up of five main parts: the Pentateuch which is the first five books of the Bible (Genesis through Deuteronomy), the Historical Books (Joshua through Esther), Psalms and Wisdom Literature (Job through Song of Songs), the Major Prophets (Isaiah, Jeremiah, and Ezekiel) and the Minor Prophets (Lamentations and Daniel through Malachi).

The New Testament is also made up of five main parts: Gospels (Matthew through John), Acts, Pauline Epistles (Romans through Philemon), General Epistles (Hebrews through Jude), and Revelation.

Jesus said, in essence, "All Scripture points to me." This is helpful for us because anytime you are reading a passage of Scripture, even if it's confusing, you can ask, "**How does this point to Jesus?**" And you will be asking the right question!

How does this change the way that you will read Scripture?..

....

The writer of Hebrews said this about Jesus: "The Son is the radiance of God's glory and the exact representation of his being, sustaining all things by his powerful word" (Hebrews 1:3).

Jesus came to change our lives. When we read Scripture under his direction, he lovingly and strongly guides us into a new way of life.

Instead of praying my prayer, I want to pray over you the prayer the Apostle Paul prayed for the new followers of Jesus in Colossians 1:9–18:

9 For this reason, since the day we heard about you, we have not stopped praying for you and asking God to fill you with the knowledge of his will through all spiritual wisdom and understanding. 10 And we pray this in order that you may live a life worthy of the Lord and may please him in every way: bearing fruit in every good work, growing in the knowledge of God, 11 being strengthened with all power according to his glorious might so that you may have great endurance and patience, and joyfully 12 giving thanks to the Father, who has qualified you to share in the inheritance of the saints in the kingdom of light.

13 For he has rescued us from the dominion of darkness and brought
us into the kingdom of the Son he loves, 14 in whom we have redemp-
tion, the forgiveness of sins. 15 He is the image of the invisible God,
the firstborn over all creation. 16 For by him all things were created:
things in heaven and on earth, visible and invisible, whether thrones
or powers or rulers or authorities; all things were created by him and
for him. 17 He is before all things, and in him all things hold together.
18 And he is the head of the body, the church; he is the beginning and
the firstborn from among the dead, so that in everything he might
have the supremacy.

I look forward to hearing the stories of how God changes your life through the power of his Word.

NOTES

learn to OVERCOME TEMPTATION

"Therefore ________ ___ ______ these ______ of _____ and _____ _____ into _______ is like a _____ _____ who _____ his ______ on the ____. The _____ ____ ____, the ______ _____, and the _____ _____ and ____ against that _____; yet it ____ ___ ____, because ____ ___ ___ _________ on the ____." Matthew 7:__-__

"Therefore everyone who hears these words of mine and puts them into practice is like a wise man who built his house on the rock. The rain came down, the streams rose, and the winds blew and beat against that house; yet it did not fall, because it had its foundation on the rock." Matthew 7:24–25

Read: Matthew 4:1–11

I find it very encouraging that Jesus doesn't just talk about what people ought to do. He shows us how to live and then tells us to do the same. In Matthew 4, Jesus was led by the Spirit into the desert to be tempted by the devil. Do you want to know how to handle temptation? Do you want to know how to succeed every time when you are tempted? Take a look at Jesus.

Jesus was tempted in three ways. According to Matthew 4:2–3, what was the first temptation about?

....

What are some ways you are tempted by normal human appetites?..

....

How did Jesus overcome this temptation?..

....

If your Bible has references (notes in the margins or at the bottom of the pages), you will see a note to let you know Jesus quoted Deuteronomy 8:3. When Jesus was tempted to use divine power to meet his own physical needs, he remembered the biblical principle that God is responsible for sustaining us by his Word. We exist because God said it. We are here by God and for God, not the other way around! We need to surrender even our human appetites to God. He will meet them in his way and at his time. It is all a gift from him. Jesus knew this principle because he knew the Word of God. It was in his heart and mind so he did not sin when tempted to do his own thing.

According to Matthew 4:5–6, what did the devil tempt Jesus to do?..

....

How did the devil try to convince Jesus he should do this?..

Isn't it amazing that the devil even used Scripture on Jesus? The devil knows how powerful Scripture is, but he did something that you should see. He quoted Scripture to make it say what he wanted it to say rather than what God intended it to mean. He cleverly quoted a portion of Psalm 91 out of context, "For he will command his angels concerning you to guard you…they will lift you up in their hands, so that you will not strike your foot against a stone" (v. 11–12). In context, however, Psalm 91:9 states, "If you make the Most High your dwelling…then no harm will befall you." God's protection comes when we live for him, not when we do foolish things. Be careful to read Scripture for what it says, not what you want it to say!

Notice again that Jesus quoted Scripture to respond to the devil's temptation. See if you can find in the marginal reference in your Bible which passage Jesus quoted.[1] Jesus was tempted to prove he was the Son of God by doing a spectacular sign. God never shows off. Asking God to do that is way out of line. Jesus knew that, because he knew the Word of God, and he could quote it when tempted. You can do the same as you learn God's Word.

What was the main topic of the devil's third temptation for Jesus according to Matthew 4:8–9?........

....

Jesus knew he would have to suffer and die a cruel death in order to save the whole world. All he had do was bow down one time to the devil, and he could have the glory without the cross. There are no shortcuts to the will of God! Jesus knew that because he knew the Word of God. We were created to worship only God. It is in these verses we find our example for how to handle temptation. We need to know the truth of God's Word in context so we can apply it to our lives.

There are no shortcuts to following Jesus and to being able to handle temptations when they come. You need to know the truth of God's Word in context. You need daily infusions of God's Word to be able to live the life God has for you. How is your Bible reading going?

Lord, thank you for your Word that teaches me how to live and to overcome temptation. I would not be able to know you personally if it were not for Jesus Christ. His example and your Word in context shows what you are like and what you think. Thanks for sending both to me to show me the way back to you. Help me to prioritize reading and applying your Word to my life daily. Amen.

....

....

....

....

....

NOTES

learn to BE PRODUCTIVE

"Therefore everyone who hears these words of mine and puts them into practice is like a wise man who built his house on the rock. The rain came down, the streams rose, and the winds blew and beat against that house; yet it did not fall, because it had its foundation on the rock." Matthew 7:24–25

Read: Luke 8:5–15

When I (Claude) was a child, we had a vegetable garden in our backyard. The only thing that I loved more than the anticipation of something growing was the moment that the vegetables were ripe enough to be picked and eaten!

There are several keys to a productive garden. You need the right seeds or starter plants, the right amount of water and sun, protection from pests, and good soil. Many people know about the first three but fail to make sure the soil is prepared properly. It is amazing how much more can be produced if you prepare the soil properly before you plant.

Jesus taught in Luke 8 how the soil of our hearts makes all the difference in our productivity as his followers. What four types of soil did Jesus describe?..

....

He taught about four kinds of heart soils: hard ground, rocky soil, thorny soil, and good soil. Each soil receives the same seed, has the same amount of water and sunlight, and the same exposure to pests, but some never produce at all. Some start to produce but don't make it, some look pretty good but never produce, and others produce greatly. The only difference is the soil.

What does Jesus say is the seed? (Luke 8:11)..

What keeps the soil on the path from producing? (Luke 8:12)..

What keeps the rocky soil from producing? (Luke 8:13)..

What keeps the thorny soil from producing? (Luke 8:14)...

What are the characteristics of the person's heart soil that produces greatly? (Luke 8:15).................

....

What does the parable of the soil help you identify that is keeping you from being productive in your walk with Jesus? What do you feel the Lord is telling you to do about it?..

....

God's word will change your life if you are willing to tend the soil of your heart. One of the biggest challenges that many Americans face is the thorn of materialism. Some exchange many things (time, energy, sleep, even relationships) so they can own the newest things or have the stuff their friends have. Jesus says our productivity in the kingdom of God can be choked out by worries, riches, and pleasures. God's plan for your life is that you would be a productive follower of Jesus, that your life would count big time for his kingdom. This would be a great time to tell the Lord that you want to surrender your desires and your resources to him. The One who made you knows how to make your life productive. Wouldn't it be a shame to live your whole life and never fulfill the reason why you are here? Wouldn't it be sad to live your life for things that won't matter five seconds after you die? I don't want to do that. I want to hear my Lord say to me one day, "Well done, good and faithful servant." I'm sure you do as well.

Take a few minutes right now to write out some things you need to adjust. When you have done that, talk to God about each item. Ask him to show you how to cultivate your heart's soil so you produce a hundredfold for him.

....

Talk to your spiritual coach about what you feel God is directing you to change. Ask how following Jesus has made a difference in his or her priorities in life. Listen for some valuable insights into how to align your life to God's values.

NOTES

QUALITY 2 RESOURCES

Bible Study Process

Choose a Passage (usually a paragraph) of Scripture you would like to study (I recommend starting with Philippians). The main thing to consider when studying Scripture is "context." Reading something in context simply means that you purpose to understand what comes before and after the passage you are studying. Not doing this results in people coming to the wrong conclusion as to what the Scripture is actually saying...they take it "out of context."

Read: Read the whole chapter that the passage you selected is in. If the passage is at the beginning of a chapter I recommend you also read the previous chapter. If the passage is at the end, then also read the chapter following. On www.youversion.com you can read the passage in multiple translations by clicking on the "parallel" button.

Look: Because of technology, the world is at your fingertips. If you don't have any commentaries available to you, you can go to: www.BibleStudyTools.com, "browse their library" and find *Matthew Henry's Complete Commentary*, Bible dictionaries, and encyclopedias for free. This is a great way to dig deeper into the passage you are studying.

Apply: As a result of understanding what this passage meant to its original hearers, how will your life be different? How does the truth of this passage affect your life today? If you're not sure..."look" more...still unsure? Bring your questions to your spiritual coach and ask how he or she would apply the passage to his or her life.

Pray: Once you understand the passage in context and see how it applies to your life, pray that God would lead change in your life in that area. Remember, you are following Jesus not just trying to change your behavior!

QUALITY 2 ▹ DECISIONS, NOTES, PRAYERS...

COACH'S SECTION

Relate
What was the best part of your week?

Review
How was your time with God this week?

What challenges, if any, did you have in spending time with God?

How are you enjoying the small group that you found? (Skip this question if you're still helping this person connect with a group or if your youth ministry doesn't currently have small groups available.)

Do you still remember Matthew 11:28–30?

> 28 "Come to me, all you who are weary and burdened, and I will give you rest. 29 Take my yoke upon you and learn from me, for I am gentle and humble in heart, and you will find rest for your souls. 30 For my yoke is easy and my burden is light." Matthew 11:28–30

How is Matthew 7:24–25 coming?

> 24 "Therefore everyone who hears these words of mine and puts them into practice is like a wise man who built his house on the rock. 25 The rain came down, the streams rose, and the winds blew and beat against that house; yet it did not fall, because it had its foundation on the rock." Matthew 7:24–25

Reflect

What stood out to you this week in your reading?

Refocus

How are you going to incorporate Bible reading into your life?

What, if any, specific questions do you have about God?

Note: Listen but don't give answers if you don't have them. If there are questions you don't have the answer to, commit to finding the answer.

What are some things you need to adjust so you can be more productive for God?

What are some obstacles you face in making that adjustment?

Resource

How can you make happen what you've decided needs to happen?

Would you like some accountability around that?

What would accountability look like for you?

Prayer

How can I pray for you this week?

Note: Turn to the prayer list you started for this person.

Ask if God has answered their requests from the previous week.

Pray for what they asked and that God would bless them in their next steps as a follower of Christ.

Set and/or confirm the date and time for the next meeting.

QUALITY 3

LEARN TO HEAL

learn to HEA

Healing is available because of what Christ did on the cross. Part of following Jesus is learning that God is able to heal. That may mean that you pray a prayer of faith for someone to be healed or believing God for your own healing. Either way, anticipate God doing things that you can't!

When I (Daniel) was in college I lifted weights to try to improve my athletic performance. One day when I went into lift, I saw a bar with more weight than I had ever lifted on the bottom of a squat rack. For some reason and without warming up (I have no idea what I was thinking), I decided to get under it and try to move it. When I pushed for all I was worth, I heard a popping/ripping sound in my lower abdomen. I went to see our doctor, and sure enough, I had a hernia. Stupid, stupid, stupid! He suggested operating right away but I talked him out of it. The basketball season was only a few weeks away and an operation would keep me out of action for about two months. I had to go back to him several times throughout the season. Each time he confirmed my hernia was getting larger. I was able to limp my way through the season, but I planned on having the surgery during spring break. A week or so before spring break, we had special meetings at the college and the speaker encouraged us to pray for healing if we needed it. I stood to be prayed for. A student placed his hand on my shoulder and asked God to heal me. I thought I felt something warm on the spot of my hernia but I didn't tell anyone. I wasn't sure so I said nothing and continued with the plan for the surgery. I went to the surgeon a day before the surgery. He checked me and he could not find the hernia. He was pretty frustrated because he had planned on a surgery and it wasn't needed! I heard him call the general practitioner and ask him why he sent me. After that phone call, I told the surgeon that I believed I was healed. He just looked at me, but I could tell that was way outside his box. He sent me back to my general practitioner who was baffled. I felt obligated to tell him that I thought I was healed. He said something like, "Prayer is a good thing." I was able to return immediately to full athletic activities, including weight lifting, without a problem. God healed me!

HEALING IS AVAILABLE BECAUSE OF WHAT CHRIST DID ON THE CROSS.

I told you that story for a couple of reasons. First, you need to know that a rational, twenty-first century human being believes he experienced a miracle. Hernias don't heal themselves. The doctor had diagnosed and confirmed I had a hernia multiple times that year. Second, healings don't always happen immediately. I prayed for my hernia to be healed many times before God did it. I don't understand why God heals some immediately, some later, and some never at all. For example, although God has healed me (Claude) in other ways, he did not heal *my* hernia (it should be noted that I was lifting at least twice what Daniel was lifting when he got his...ha ha ha). The fact remains, the Bible teaches us that God heals and he invites us to ask.

Throughout this quality, as you read a variety of miracle stories, it's our hope that you will not only be open to God being active in your life, but that your faith would grow. If there is a God and if he is as the Bible describes, then God can suspend natural laws at any time to do the supernatural! Jesus said,

Ask and it will be given to you; seek and you will find; knock and the door will be opened to you. For everyone who asks receives; he who seeks finds; and to him who knocks, the door will be opened. (Matthew 7:7–8)

Ask.

Creator, you spoke and the world came into existence out of nothing. You said, "Let there be light," and there was light. That is so far beyond anything I can understand. Show me the truth about healing, and from this moment on, I want everything you have for me. Amen.

NOTES

learn the IMPORTANCE OF TOUCH

"Ask and it will be given to you; seek and you will find; knock and the door will be opened to you. For everyone who asks receives; he who seeks finds; and to him who knocks, the door will be opened." Matthew 7:7–8

◃ MEMORIZE SCRIPTURE

Scripture Memory Review: Matthew 11:28–30; Matthew 7:24–25

Read: Matthew 4:18–22

The first thing Jesus did after calling his disciples to follow him was to invite them to hear him teach about God's kingdom and to watch him heal people...that is significant! From the beginning, they would know that when Jesus is around, anything is possible. Matthew 4:23–24 reads this way:

> *Jesus went throughout Galilee, teaching in their synagogues, preaching the good news of the kingdom, and healing every disease and sickness among the people. News about him spread all over Syria, and people brought to him all who were ill with various diseases, those suffering severe pain, the demon-possessed, those having seizures, and the paralyzed, and he healed them.*

How do you think it might have affected the early disciples to see Jesus healing people?..................

....

According to a survey conducted by Time Magazine, 69 percent of Americans believe in miracles.[1]

Do you believe in miracles? Why or why not?..

....

There are a lot of miracles recorded in the Bible, but one moves me emotionally more than the rest.

Read Matthew 8:1–4.

I'm moved by this story on several levels. First, the man was desperate. There was no known cure for leprosy. They no doubt thought about it much like we think of cancer or HIV. However, lepers were required to live outside the community! They also had to communicate they were diseased by how they dressed, and they had to keep to themselves (Leviticus 13:45–46; Numbers 5:1–4). In addition, sometimes leprosy was a direct punishment from God (Numbers 12:10; 2 Kings 5:27). The average person wanted nothing to do with a leper for obvious reasons. Somehow the man in Matthew 8 heard about Jesus. He came and knelt before Jesus and said, "...if you are willing, you can make me clean." The depth of need, the humility, the hope demonstrated, all move me. But I think it is the next thing that moves me the most. "Jesus reached out his hand and touched the man." What? Jesus touched the man with the skin disease? Yes, Jesus touched someone who hadn't been touched in who knows how long, perhaps in years. Jesus' heart broke for someone who was alone, an outcast, without a place to belong; one whose body was riddled with disease. He touched him. That's what God is like. His heart is moved by our brokenness. He knows what we are going through, the visible and the invisible, and he cares. The man was not just another notch in Jesus' healing belt. The man with leprosy was a person with a broken life who needed to be touched by his Creator.

There is one more thing about the story that moves me: the humility of the leprous man. He didn't stay away from Jesus; he was not passive. He did not demand that Jesus heal him. He simply believed Jesus could do it, he knelt before him in humility, and he asked.

This story impacts me because I have broken places in my life that I would like Jesus to touch. Some of them are easy to see but others aren't. I'm guessing that you have them too. Even though it's still a mystery why some people are healed and others aren't, this story shows me what God is like. He sees our brokenness. He cares. As we come to him, he reaches out and touches us in our diseased state. God is not a distant, impersonal, and unapproachable force in the universe. God is a person who reaches out to us in our need. He knows what we need and he is moved by it.

What comes to your mind when you read this description about Jesus?...

....

What areas of your life do you need Jesus to touch?..

....

Take a few minutes to talk with Jesus about it right now.

Jesus, my Healer, when you were on this earth you saw people's need and your heart was moved by their suffering. Right now I bring myself to you like the man in Matthew 8. I cannot demand anything. I present my need before you. (Talk with Jesus now about your need even though he already knows.) Would you stretch out your hand and touch me in my need? I realize that you are here and that I am not alone in this. I trust your Word that says that in all things you work for the good of those who love you (Romans 8:28). I do love you and I ask you to have your way in my life. Amen.

Receiving Jesus' Touch Through Others

You may decide to share the area of your life that needs healing with your spiritual coach or your small group. We weren't designed to suffer alone. Jesus created us to be in community with others to "rejoice with those who rejoice" and to "mourn with those who mourn" (Romans 12:15), and to help "carry each other's burdens" (Galatians 6:2). That means you are not alone! Regardless of how we got to where we are, God will help us carry our burdens through his people. He may not remove our consequences. The law of sowing and reaping is part of the laws he set up in the universe. But he will help us. One way he helps us is through his people. It's humbling but it is right and it is good. I encourage you to share what you're going through with other followers of Jesus. You won't be sorry!

learn to RECOGNIZE JESUS' AUTHORITY

"Ask and it __________ to you; seek and __________; knock and the door __________ to you. For everyone who asks ________; he who seeks ____; and to him who ______, the door will be ______." ________ 7:7–8

MEMORIZE SCRIPTURE ◂

"Ask and it will be given to you; seek and you will find; knock and the door will be opened to you. For everyone who asks receives; he who seeks finds; and to him who knocks, the door will be opened." Matthew 7:7–8

Read: Matthew 8:5–13

In this story, a Roman military officer who was in charge of a hundred men (a centurion) came to Jesus in Capernaum to let Jesus know that his servant was paralyzed and in terrible trouble. Jesus said to him, "I will go and heal him." Several things about this surprise me. First, the man is not a Jew. The average Jew hated the Roman occupation and wanted nothing to do with any Roman citizens, especially the soldiers. Somehow, the centurion knew Jesus was above all that, that Jesus cared for everyone, even those who have professions we have no respect for. Jesus obviously had a reputation of caring for everyone. So, this man came to the One who offered hope.

The second thing that surprises me is that Jesus offered to go and heal the man's servant without being asked. Jesus is proactive with his healing. When he hears a need, he responds. This surprises the centurion. He knows the social separation between Jews and Romans. Jews did not enter the homes of non-Jews because they thought it made them unclean. But Jesus was going to go anyway. Why? Because people matter to God. You matter to God! God isn't held back by traditions and social rules that separate people from God. Isn't that great news? Jesus proactively goes to where the needs are.

Furthermore, the centurion is a man of great faith. The centurion tells Jesus he doesn't deserve to have Jesus come to his house. Instead, the centurion explains his understanding of authority and then suggests that Jesus could just "say the word" and heal his servant without coming for a visit. The man's faith astonished Jesus and me as well. The man believed Jesus could heal from long distance.

This is exactly what Jesus did. "Jesus said to the centurion, 'Go! It will be done just as you believed it would.' And his servant was healed at that very hour."

As you are learning about healing, you need to know that Jesus cares about people wherever they are found, that he is proactive, and that he responds to faith. The centurion put himself in a position to receive a miracle by believing that Jesus cared and that he could do it.

How does this story impact your life?..

....

How might a person put themselves in a position to receive a miracle?..

....

As you read God's Word and observe how Jesus heals people, your faith in God will grow. Faith is simply believing that Jesus cares and that he can do it. It is confident trust.

Do you believe Jesus can heal now? Why or why not?...

....

If you struggle with faith, you are not alone. You might be like Thomas, one of the twelve disciples, who struggled with his faith. After Jesus' resurrection, some of the disciples saw Jesus when Thomas wasn't around. When Thomas heard about it, he refused to believe. His words are recorded in John 20:25: "Unless I see the nail marks in his hands and put my finger where the nails were, and put my hand into his side, I will not believe it." A week later, Jesus appeared to Thomas. He told Thomas to touch his hands and his side and then he said, "Stop doubting and believe." Jesus wasn't upset that Thomas struggled with his faith. He gave him clear information, but he also knew that Thomas needed to make an informed decision to believe.

You might be like the father who was described in Mark 9:14–32 whose son was being tormented by an evil spirit. When the father brought his son to Jesus, "Jesus said, 'Everything is possible for him who believes.' Immediately the boy's father exclaimed, 'I do believe; help me overcome my unbelief!'" (Mark 9:23–24). You may believe but you may also doubt. Bring all that to the Lord and ask him to help you with it.

Take some time right now to talk with the Lord about your needs. While you are at it, ask him for help with your faith as well. He can grow your ability to have confident trust in him.

Lord, I'm amazed and humbled to know that nothing can keep you from caring about my life. You have been reaching out to me my whole life! Even though I didn't always respond, you continued to pursue me. I am so grateful for that. I believe you can do anything. Increase my faith. Replace my doubts with faith. Show yourself to me in unmistakable ways. (Take the time right now to present your needs to God. Ask him to heal or meet your need. Then, tell God you trust him with his decision.) Thank you for your unfailing love. I need you in my life today. Amen.

learn that HEALING IS GOD'S IDEA

"Ask ______ ______ ______ ______ ______ to ___; seek ______ ______ ______ ______; knock ______ ______ ______

______ ______ ______ to ___. For ______ ______ asks ______; he ______ ______ ______;

___ ___ him ______ ______, ______ ______ ______ ______ ______ ______." ______:7–8

MEMORIZE SCRIPTURE ◂

"Ask and it will be given to you; seek and you will find; knock and the door will be opened to you. For everyone who asks receives; he who seeks finds; and to him who knocks, the door will be opened." Matthew 7:7–8

Read: Matthew 8:14–17

The next miracle Jesus performed was to heal Peter's mother-in-law. This healing was a great move on Jesus' part because she was then able to wait on everyone. (Don't get upset. I'm just having some fun.) After that healing, many people were brought to Jesus to be delivered and healed. Don't miss the explanation in verse 17: "This was to fulfill what was spoken through the prophet Isaiah: 'He took up our infirmities and carried our diseases.'"

This is a direct quote of Isaiah 53. The book of Isaiah was written about seven hundred years before Jesus was born. Throughout the book there are hints of a leader who would come to change the course of history and bring peace. Isaiah 53:4–5 describes a suffering servant who would bring healing:

> *Surely he took up our infirmities and carried our sorrows, yet we considered him stricken by God, smitten by him and afflicted. But he was pierced for our transgressions, he was crushed for our iniquities; the punishment that brought us peace was upon him, and by his wounds we are healed.*

The early followers of Jesus were Jewish. They knew about this prophecy, and they rightly linked its fulfillment to Jesus. Isaiah 53 also describes the suffering servant pouring out his life unto death, bearing the sin of many, and interceding for people who are far from God. These were also fulfilled in Jesus.

I'm telling you all this because I want you to see that it is in the nature of God to heal and restore people. It is God's idea, not ours, that healing takes place. The One who spoke the world into existence can say the word and bring healing to your life!

God still heals bodies and does miracles, but the greatest miracle that will ever take place in your life is God healing your soul. Quoting from Isaiah 53:9, the Apostle Peter explains this in 1 Peter 2:22: "He committed no sin, and no deceit was found in his mouth." He then provided the following explanation in verses 23–25:

> *When they hurled their insults at him, he did not retaliate; when he suffered, he made no threats. Instead, he entrusted himself to him who judges justly. He himself bore our sins in his body on the tree, so that we might die to sins and live for righteousness; by his wounds*

you have been healed. For you were like sheep going astray, but now you have returned to the Shepherd and Overseer of your souls.

We who were once far away from God, can now be close to God because Jesus paid the debt of our sins on the cross. Because Jesus did that, God can heal our souls. Why not take a few minutes right now to thank God that Jesus died for your sins and brought healing to your soul. Then, ask him to also heal your body or mind…ask!

Heavenly Father, cause my faith to grow. I want to believe you can do anything. Thank you for healing my soul by sending Jesus to bear my sins on the cross. I know I can't earn your love. Jesus has already earned it for me. I just accept what you did for me and I thank you. Thank you for making me new on the inside. Continue to heal me in every area of my life as well. (Take a few minutes now and tell the Lord about other areas of your life that need his healing touch. Pour out your heart to the Lord and trust him with the results.)

One final thought: healing may or may not come like you expect. But God does all things well. He is with you and you can trust him. He is always good and he is always loving.

learn to ASK IN FAITH

SCRIPTURE ◃

"____ ____ ____ ____ ____ given ____ ____; seek ____ ____ ____ ____; ____ ____ ____ ____ door ____ ____ ____ ____ ____ ____. ____ everyone ____ ____ receives; ____ ____ ____ finds; ____ ____ ____ ____ knocks, ____ ____ ____ ____ ____." ____ 7:_-_

"Ask and it will be given to you; seek and you will find; knock and the door will be opened to you. For everyone who asks receives; he who seeks finds; and to him who knocks, the door will be opened." Matthew 7:7–8

Read: Matthew 9:1–8

I hope you have seen by now the connection between miracles and faith. Read Matthew 9:2 again closely.

Whose faith moved Jesus to heal the man?..

If you said the men who carried the paralytic to Jesus, you are correct. It always inspires me when I read about their faith. They carried their friend to Jesus because they believed Jesus could heal him. This has huge implications for followers of Jesus. You may have friends who aren't sure if God can heal them, but you can bring them to Jesus anyway. As you listen and care for those around you, you will hear stories of heartache and pain, some physical and otherwise. After you care for your friends and if you listen thoroughly to them, you may want to ask, "Do you mind if I pray for you?" Most friends will say, "That would be fine." Sometimes people will say, "No, thanks." Don't be discouraged by that. But if they do agree, find a quiet place off to the side or in a parking lot or wherever it seems appropriate and bring their need to Jesus. Sometimes you will not pray for them at that time but later. The point is that you will want to ask God on their behalf to heal them. Being there for your friend this way may be something new; if you're unsure what that could look like, your prayer can be something like this, "Heavenly Father, I bring [say his name] to you right now. He needs you to bring healing in [name the area] of his life. You spoke and the world came into existence. You have intervened many times and changed the course of history. I believe you can do it again. I ask you now to just say the word and heal [name]. We promise to give you all the honor and the glory for the healing. In Jesus' name we pray, amen." If you begin to ask God for healing, you will begin to see his supernatural intervention in your life and in the lives of those around you. It's pretty cool that God responds to our asking.

I want you to notice something else about this particular story. *What did Jesus say after he saw their faith?*..

....

Does his response surprise you? I was expecting him to say, "Rise up and walk" but he says instead, "Take heart, son; your sins are forgiven." The rest of the story explains why Jesus did that. He wanted everyone to know that he cannot only heal our bodies, more importantly, he heals souls. He did say, "Get up, take your mat and go home." And the man did that and went home. The people praised God because of what Jesus did.

It is an awesome thing that Jesus is able to heal the whole person. God has changed and is continuing to change your life; he will change the lives of everyone who asks. Ultimately and in God's timing, we are all going to die a physical death. But when Jesus heals our souls by forgiving our sins, we will live forever with God. I love the verse in 1 John 1:9, "If we confess our sins, he is faithful and just and will forgive us our sins and purify us from all unrighteousness."

Take a few minutes right now to thank God for healing your soul by forgiving your sins. I encourage you also to take a few minutes to begin praying for the needs of your friends. What a wonderful privilege it is to present your friends' needs to the one who holds the whole world in his hands. I won't write out a prayer for you this time. Just use your own words to communicate with God.

learn to GIVE IT AWAY

MEMORIZE SCRIPTURE ▹

"_____ _____ _____ _____ _____ _____ _____ _____; _____ _____ _____ _____ _____; _____ _____ _____ _____

_____ _____ _____ _____ _____. _____ _____ _____ _____ _____; _____ _____ _____ _____;

_____ _____ _____ _____ _____, _____ _____ _____ _____ _____." _____ _____:_–_

"Ask and it will be given to you; seek and you will find; knock and the door will be opened to you. For everyone who asks receives; he who seeks finds; and to him who knocks, the door will be opened." Matthew 7:7–8

Read: Matthew 10:1–8

I have often wondered how it must have felt to be a follower of Jesus in person. It would have been amazing to see him perform miracles and to hear him speak. When you read this passage you see his plan that his followers would do as he did: preach the nearness of God's kingdom and perform miracles.

How would you have felt if Jesus said to you, "I give you authority to drive out evil spirits and to heal every disease and sickness"?..

I would have felt inadequate, excited, humbled, and hopeful at the same time. The fact remains, we can do nothing apart from Christ and his authority. The most encouraging words to me are found in Matthew 10:8, "Freely you have received, freely give." Jesus expects us to give away what he has given to us. Gifts that we receive are to be used, not hoarded.

There are plenty of examples in the New Testament of how God healed people because of the prayers of the disciples via the power of the Holy Spirit. One example is found in Acts 3. Read Acts 3:1–10.

What stands out to you about this story?..

....

Praying for people to be healed is only giving away what God gives you. I (Claude) was about three years into youth ministry when a very upset mother approached me after a youth service. She explained that she had a severed relationship with a child and wanted to repair it but was too hurt over the things that were done and said. After she shared the details of the situation, my heart was broken as she concluded by asking for my advice as a youth pastor. I had no words of wisdom. I looked at her and said, "I haven't been where you are and can't imagine the pain that you feel, but God knows what you're going through and I feel led to pray for healing for you. Is that okay with you?" She had a strange look on her face (it wasn't the response she was looking for) but agreed that she needed some emotional healing. I prayed a very simple prayer and God did something in her heart...after her tears, she explained that she knew exactly what needed to be said to her daughter. No advice, just prayer. She needed to experience an emotional healing in order to see the answer that God had already provided in her situation. From that moment on, I've always started those conversations with prayer for healing, and countless times the answer is provided after an emotional healing and before my advice is given. So many times our default thought is that healing is available physically but God heals us mentally, spiritually, and emotionally as well! God wants to heal you and others; ask.

Read 1 Corinthians 12:4–11. It is really important to remember that God is always the hero. He just lets us be a part of the miracle. Reread 1 Corinthians 12:6.

Who is it who works gifts in all men?...

That's right! It's God and not us. We are just instruments through whom God works. It amazes me that God includes us in his work. He could just do it on his own but he lets us be part of it. That amazes me! I also want you to notice 1 Corinthians 12:9. Notice that "gifts" is plural. In other words, there is more than one gift of healing. God can do anything he wants through any of us. If the Spirit of God is in you, then the same God who spoke the world into existence can do great things through you! He is the same God. I have come to realize, however, that God tends to use some people more in one area of healing and other people in other areas. For example, I have prayed for many people over the years and have witnessed different types of healing, but God has used me more often when I pray for emotional healing in parent-child situations. I'm not sure why that is, but I'm thankful.

I need to address one last thing before we move on: the question, "Why does God heal one thing and not another?" Whole books are written on this subject.[1] I (Claude) already shared in *First Steps: Youth Edition* how God had healed my knee after a very serious injury, yet as I mentioned earlier, he didn't heal my hernia. I prayed several times for a healing touch from the same God that had healed me less than a year earlier but surgery was required. There are some who say we are not healed because of lack of faith. There is certainly a link between lack of faith and lack of healing. Matthew 13:58 describes what happened when Jesus went to his hometown, "And he did not do many miracles there because of their lack of faith." We need to be careful not to judge, however, because sometimes people have faith but God chooses not to heal. When this happens, one thing is certain. God's character never changes. Ten times in the Bible God is described as a "compassionate and gracious God, slow to anger and abounding in love" (Exodus 34:6; 2 Chronicles 30:9; Nehemiah 9:17; Psalms 86:15, 103:8, 111:4, 112:4, 145:8; Joel 2:13; Jonah 4:2). In other words, **God's choice to heal one and not another is not based on his love and compassion for an individual**. God is always loving and he always cares for you. When he chooses not to heal, I have two recommendations. *First, trust him.* Don't freak out and turn your back on him in anger. He is your best friend. Even if you turn your back on him, he will never turn his back on you. He loves you and you can trust him. *Second, look for the good in the situation*. You may not see it right away, you may never see it, but look for it anyway. I have clung to the truth of Romans 8:28 when life doesn't make sense: "And we know that in all things God works for the good of those who love him, who have been called according to his purpose." It doesn't say that "all things are good."

...ONE THING IS CERTAIN. GOD'S CHARACTER NEVER CHANGES.

It says that "in all things God works for the good of those who love him." So, ask God for healing; believe that he can heal; experience healing, and trust him when he chooses to not heal. This was a longer section today with a lot of information to digest. Take advantage of the notes area at the end of this quality to write any thoughts and questions you might have. Please read the prayer below and realize I'm praying for you...

Heavenly Father, thank you for your kindness in our lives. I am encouraged today, even while I am writing this, that your character never changes, that you are a gracious and compassionate God, slow to anger and abounding in love. We have been through a lot together, and you have always been kind to me. Even when you have allowed me to go through painful things, both physically and emotionally, you have been there for me. Allow every individual who reads this book to learn that about you as well. Help them to cling to you in times of joy and sorrow, when you heal and when you choose to do things differently from what we ask. Teach my friends to rejoice in you at all times and to find your corresponding peace because of it (Philippians 4:4–7). We need you at every turn in our lives. Give my friends faith to believe you are "able to do immeasurably more than all we ask or imagine, according to [your] power that is at work within us, to [you] be glory in the church and in Christ Jesus throughout all generations, for ever and ever! Amen" (Ephesians 3:20–21).

Conflict Resolution Process[1]

Overview of Conflict

1. It is a normal part of life.
2. Provides an opportunity to grow.
3. We decide how we are going to handle conflict.

Problem Solving Process

1. Pray to get your own heart right before you do anything.
   - Do not proceed until you know before God that you love the other person and want God's best for them.
2. Set a time and place for discussion.
   - Make sure you set aside adequate time.
   - Choose a place to talk where you will not be interrupted.
3. Define the problem or issue of disagreement.
   - Select one issue at a time.
   - Define the issue in a way that is mutually agreeable.
4. How do each of you contribute to the problem?
   - The purpose is to discover how the problem evolved in order to find a solution.
5. List past attempts to resolve the issue that were not successful.
6. Brainstorm about possible solutions.
   - The purpose of this is to generate fresh ideas without attempting to evaluate their relative merits.
7. Discuss and evaluate the possible solutions.
8. Agree on one solution and try.

- To agree upon a choice does not always mean it is the first choice of either partner.

9. Agree on how each individual will work toward this solution.
   - Be specific and focus on observable behaviors.
10. Set up another meeting to discuss your progress.
    - Set the meeting reasonably soon (i.e., one week from now).
    - Partners can discuss the degree to which the plan is working and in which to further their progress.
11. Reward each other as you each contribute toward the solution.
    - Watch for ways in which your partner positively contributes to resolving the conflict.
    - Encourage and praise one another for their efforts.

Grief Process[2]

1. Shock stage: Initial paralysis at hearing the bad news.
2. Denial stage: Frustrated outpouring of bottled-up emotion.
3. Bargaining stage: Seeking in vain for a way out.
4. Depression stage: Final realization of the inevitable.
5. Testing stage: Seeking realistic solutions.
6. Acceptance stage: Finally finding the way forward.

12 Step Recovery Process with Scripture References[3]

Step 1–We admitted we were powerless over our addictions and compulsive behaviors, that our lives had become unmanageable.

I know that nothing good lives in me, that is, in my sinful nature. For I have the desire to do what is good, but I cannot carry it out. Romans 7:18

Step 2–We came to believe that a power greater than ourselves could restore us to sanity.

For it is God who works in you to will and to act according to his good purpose. Philippians 2:13

Step 3–We made a decision to turn our lives and our wills over to the care of God.

Therefore, I urge you, brothers, in view of God's mercy, to offer your bodies as living sacrifices, holy and pleasing to God–this is your spiritual act of worship. Romans 12:1

Step 4–We made a searching and fearless moral inventory of ourselves.

Let us examine our ways and test them, and let us return to the Lord. Lamentations 3:40

Step 5–We admitted to God, to ourselves, and to another human being the exact nature of our wrongs.

Therefore confess your sins to each other and pray for each other so that you may be healed. James 5:16

Step 6–We were entirely ready to have God remove all these defects of character.

Humble yourselves before the Lord, and he will lift you up. James 4:10

Step 7–We humbly asked Him to remove all our shortcomings.

If we confess our sins, he is faithful and just and will forgive us our sins and purify us from all unrighteousness. 1 John 1:9

Step 8–We made a list of all persons we had harmed and became willing to make amends to them all.

Do to others as you would have them do to you. Luke 6:31

Step 9–We made direct amends to such people whenever possible, except when to do so would injure them or others.

Therefore, if you are offering your gift at the altar and there remember that your brother has something against you, leave your gift there in front of the altar. First go and be reconciled to your brother; then come and offer your gift. Matthew 5:23–24

Step 10–We continue to take personal inventory and when we were wrong, promptly admitted it.

So, if you think you are standing firm, be careful that you don't fall! 1 Corinthians 10:12

Step 11–We sought through prayer and meditation to improve our conscious contact with God, praying only for knowledge of his will for us, and power to carry that out.

Let the word of Christ dwell in you richly. Colossians 3:16

Step 12–Having had a spiritual experience as the result of these steps, we try to carry this message to others and to practice these principles in all our affairs.

Brothers, if someone is caught in a sin, you who are spiritual should restore him gently. But watch yourself, or you also may be tempted. Galatians 6:1

QUALITY 3 ▹ DECISIONS, NOTES, PRAYERS...

COACH'S SECTION

Relate

How is your week going?

Review

What's working? What's not working from your perspective?

Reflect

What stood out to you from the reading this week?

Refocus

In what area(s) of your life would you like healing?

Note: Take time to pray right now for healing.

Resource

What could you do to provide room for healing in your life?

Note: The person should know they can do the following:

Ask God to heal them (spiritually, physically, mentally and/or emotionally)

See a doctor if it is something medical

Learn about a helpful healing process (Grief, Conflict Resolution, Recovery)

What resources do you need to find healing?

Prayer

In what other ways can I pray for you this week?

Note: Turn to the prayer list you started for this person.
Ask if God has answered their requests from the previous week.

Does anyone around you need healing?

Note: Encourage them to lead in prayer for that person as you close (if they are comfortable doing so).

Pray for what they asked and that God would bless them as they take the next steps as a follower of Christ.

Set and/or confirm the date and time for the next meeting.

PRAYER REQUESTS

QUALITY 4

LEARN TO INFLUENCE

learn to INFLUENCE

I (Claude) grew up in a home where I was taught that every person is an influencer. At the age of seven we began attending a local church, and I had a front row seat to the transformation that took place in both my parents and our home. It was nothing short of a miracle to see life change that actually influenced others. Even seeing that unfold, it pales in comparison to the scale and magnitude of what occurs in the book of Acts.

As I read and reread the Gospels and Acts, three things stand out to me about influencing people for Christ. First, followers of Jesus are called to attract people to him. Jesus told his followers they are to be the salt of the earth and the light of the world (Matthew 5:13–16). Salt on food makes you want to come back for more. Light shows you the right path. Jesus embodied this. His teaching style was attractive. His personality was magnetic. The miracles he did and the way he cared for his disciples attracted people, causing them to want to follow him. He was "attractional."

Second, we need the empowerment of the Holy Spirit to be effective witnesses for Christ. After Jesus resurrected from the dead and before he ascended into heaven, Jesus told his disciples to wait until they had been empowered by the Holy Spirit (Acts 1:8). Jesus had given his followers a seemingly impossible task, "Make disciples of all nations" (Matthew 28:18–20). Think about it for a minute. There were no planes, trains, automobiles, televisions, cell phones, or Internet! All they had was a changed life and a promise that when the Holy Spirit came on them, they would have power to witness effectively. At a large Jewish celebration called Pentecost just fifty days after Jesus' resurrection, it happened. The early followers of Jesus were in prayer, waiting for the empowerment of the Holy Spirit, when a supernatural wind filled the place where they were sitting. People saw something that looked like tongues of fire that separated and rested on everyone present. Every follower of Christ present began to speak in languages they had never learned.[1] People in the street heard what was happening and were surprised to hear someone in Jerusalem praising God in their native language when their native language was not the language spoken in Jerusalem. In the middle of that scene, Peter stood to address the growing crowd. Just fifty days earlier, Peter denied being a follower of Jesus at nighttime to a servant girl. Yet in this story, he is able to stand before a crowd of thousands to challenge them to make a decision to follow Jesus. That can happen when the Holy Spirit empowers a person. It can happen to you! About three thousand people made commitments to follow Christ that day and were baptized. That's an effective day.

Third, sharing Christ is personal. One exciting thing I've discovered is there are different styles for sharing your faith that are modeled in the New Testament: confrontational, intellectual, testimonial, relational, invitational, and serving. Your style of sharing Christ will be unique to you. Each day we'll explore a different style and then ask the Holy Spirit to empower us to share Christ effectively.

Take some time right now to ask God to empower you with the Holy Spirit like he did with the early followers of Jesus so you can be the most effective witness you can be. It's not something to fear. Jesus said, "If you then,

> though you are evil, know how to give good gifts to your children, how much more will your Father in heaven give the Holy Spirit to those who ask him!" (Luke 11:13).

Don't be surprised if the Holy Spirit enables you to speak in a language you have never learned. It is not uncommon at all. In fact, it is normal and can be expected. If this whole thing is new to you or if you are uncomfortable about it, make it a matter of prayer. It should not produce anxiety in you. It is a good thing from God. He will lead you as you seek him. I have personally experienced this, and it is part of my daily prayer life with God. Feel free to talk with your spiritual coach if you have questions.

Heavenly Father, I worship you today. There is none like you. You reached out to me, accepted me, forgave me, and you are changing my life. I ask you to empower me by your Holy Spirit today like you did your early followers. Completely baptize me in the Holy Spirit. Enable me to praise you beyond my own words and understanding. I want and need your power to be the witness you are calling me to be. There are people all around me who are hungry for you. Give me the ability to share Christ with them effectively. I wait for you now to empower me. (I encourage you to be responsive now to the work of the Holy Spirit in your life. If he gives you words to pray, pray them. If he gives you words that are beyond your understanding that sound like another language, say them. It is the Holy Spirit praying through you. When the Holy Spirit enables you to pray, it is a beautiful thing.)

learn to INVITE PEOPLE

MEMORIZE SCRIPTURE ◂

"Then Jesus came to them and said, 'All authority in heaven and on earth has been given to me. Therefore go and make disciples of all nations, baptizing them in the name of the Father and of the Son and of the Holy Spirit, and teaching them to obey everything I have commanded you. And surely I am with you always, to the very end of the age.'" Matthew 28:18–20

Scripture Memory Review: Matthew 11:28–30; Matthew 7:24–25; Matthew 7:7–8

Take the Evangelism Styles Questionnaire on page 142.

Read: John 1:40–46

One of the most exciting things you will ever do is bring a friend to Jesus. The excitement is not just yours. Jesus said, "There is rejoicing in the presence of the angels of God over one sinner who repents" (Luke 15:10). But how do you "bring a friend to Jesus"?

One of the most practical ways to bring people to Christ is to literally bring people to events where they can meet Christ, to church services, concerts, parties, etc. Studies show that people are most likely to follow Christ because of the influence of a friend or family member.[1] This is especially important for you, since 64 percent of people who follow Jesus said they made the decision before they were age 18.[2]

This is exactly what you see when Andrew met Jesus. John 1:41–42 reads, "The first thing Andrew did was to find his brother Simon and tell him, 'We have found the Messiah' (that is the Christ). And he brought him to Jesus." The Apostle Peter came to Jesus because his brother brought him.

List some friends or family members you would like to introduce to Jesus.

....

....

As you look at those names, who do you think you should invite first?..................................

What are some practical ways you can invite someone to meet Jesus?..................................

....

My hope is that you feel comfortable bringing your friends and family to your youth ministry and church. Our youth ministry goes to great lengths to create an environment where everyone and anyone is welcome. Everything is done with your friends and family members in mind! We do this because we realize that you are bringing them to meet Jesus. Every week we give teenagers a non-intimidating opportunity to follow Jesus while discovering some of the deeper things of what it means for you to continue to follow him.

Do you feel free to invite your friends and family to your youth ministry and church? Why or why not?

....

What could you do in your youth ministry to make the gathering a better place to bring your friends and family?...

There are some additional steps you can take to start bringing your friends to Christ.

First, make a longer, more complete list of people who could benefit from a relationship with Jesus. There are four categories of people who are close to you. Write down who comes to your mind that you might want to introduce to Jesus:

Friends ....

Family Members ....

Classmates/Co-workers ....

Neighbors ....

Second, continue to pray for them. Jesus said in John 6:44, "No one can come to me unless the Father who sent me draws him." No one loses their free will to accept or reject Christ, but you can pray for each person in the following ways:

- Present the person to God by name as someone for whom he died.
- Ask God to pull this person to himself, to open his eyes to the emptiness of life without him.
- Ask God to help him see his need for forgiveness and to remove any confusion about God and the good life he offers.
- Ask God to help him understand the meaning and the importance of Christ's finished work on the cross.
- Ask God to open his heart to God's love and truth.

You can also pray for yourself in the following ways:

- Ask God to help you live a consistent and attractive Christian life.
- Ask God to help you be authentic and honest as you deal with life's ups and downs.
- Ask God to give you wisdom to know how to approach friends and family.
- Ask God to grant you appropriate boldness and courage to communicate his love effectively.
- Ask God to expand your knowledge so you will be ready to clearly define and communicate God's message.
- Ask God to use you as he leads this person into a relationship with him.

Take a few minutes right now to pray for the people on your list using the suggestions above to guide you.

NOTES

learn to SHARE YOUR STORY

"Then _____ came to them and ___, 'All authority in _____ and on earth ___ ____ ____ to me. _________ go and ____ disciples of all nations, baptizing ____ in the name of the _____ and of the ___ and of the Holy ____, and teaching them to ____ everything I have commanded you. And _____ I am with you always, to the very end of the age.'" _______ 28:18–20

"Then Jesus came to them and said, 'All authority in heaven and on earth has been given to me. Therefore go and make disciples of all nations, baptizing them in the name of the Father and of the Son and of the Holy Spirit, and teaching them to obey everything I have commanded you. And surely I am with you always, to the very end of the age.'" Matthew 28:18–20

Read: John 9:1–25

Everyone's story with Jesus is different. As you look back on your life, you will probably see how God has been reaching out to you through circumstances, people, and experiences. Maybe a friend or co-worker lived a different lifestyle that stood out to you and attracted you to Christ. Perhaps a friend or a family member showed you kindness or support during a difficult season in your life. While we all have the same need for forgiveness and relationship with God through Jesus, how someone becomes a follower of Christ is always unique.

There are at least four reasons why it is important for you to tell your story. First, it helps people around you know why your life is changing. Second, it brings honor to God. Although you are an important person in your story, God is really the hero. Only God can change a life! Third, it gives people hope that God can change their lives too. Fourth, it is difficult for anyone to argue with your personal experience. Don't allow your fear of questions being asked to stop you from sharing what God has done in your life. While you may not have all the answers to their questions (which is normal and okay), you can share what you do know—how Jesus has changed and is changing your life!

Based on John 9:1–2, what do you think the man's life was like before he met Jesus?......................

....

How did Jesus change his life?..

The people questioning this man were well educated and powerful. Why was his story so powerful to them even though he wasn't educated or powerful?..

Read John 9:35–38. How did this man become a believer in Jesus?...

What happened after the man believed?...

Writing Your Story

Take a few minutes now to write out your story using the following questions to guide you. Remember, Jesus is the hero of your faith story!

Where were you spiritually before receiving Christ?..

....

How did that affect you—your feelings, attitudes, actions, and relationships?..................................

....

What caused you to start considering Christ as the solution to your needs?.....................................

....

What realization did you come to that finally caused you to ask Jesus to be the leader of your life?

....

What did you do specifically to receive Christ?..

....

How has your life begun to change since you trusted Christ?..

....

What other positive things have happened in your life since becoming a follower of Christ?.............

....

What passage of Scripture means a lot to you now that you are a follower of Christ?........................

....

I have a few suggestions. First, share your story with your spiritual coach. It will be good practice even though you may have already told him or her. Second, take the time to write out your story in its entirety. If you're comfortable, I'd also like to invite you to send your story to me via e-mail at: youthfollowingjesus@gmail.com. I love hearing how God is changing young people's lives. Please let me know in that e-mail if you are comfortable with me sharing it with others. I may even post it on the website so others can rejoice in what God is doing! Third, practice telling your story in private. Say it again and again until you are comfortable sharing it. Fourth, shorten your story. Most people will listen for about three minutes without feeling overwhelmed. Less is best. Fifth, ask a friend or family member if you can share your story with him. When you are done, thank him for listening. Ask him what he thinks of your story. Tell him that if he ever wants to share his spiritual journey, you would enjoy hearing it.

Thank you, Savior, for changing my life. I know you are going to continue to change me as well. I lift my friends and family up to you right now. (Present them by name to God now.) Draw them to yourself. Use circumstances and situations to help them realize you love them and have a purpose for their lives. Help me to be an accurate witness of how you can change a life. I know I can't do that on my own. Use me to bring people to you. Amen.

learn to BE A GENUINE FRIEND

SCRIPTURE ▹

"Then _____ came to _____ and ____, 'All ________ in ______ and on _____ has ____ given to me. _________ go and _____ ________ of all ______, baptizing ____ in the _____ of the ______ and of the ____ and of the _____ _____, and teaching _____ to _____ everything I have ___________ you. And ______ I am ____ you ______, to the _____ end of the ____.'" Matthew __:18–20

"Then Jesus came to them and said, 'All authority in heaven and on earth has been given to me. Therefore go and make disciples of all nations, baptizing them in the name of the Father and of the Son and of the Holy Spirit, and teaching them to obey everything I have commanded you. And surely I am with you always, to the very end of the age.'" Matthew 28:18–20

Read: Luke 5:27–30

As I (Claude) started to try to connect with my friends in spiritual conversations, I realized I didn't know how to relate to some of them. When I began following Jesus I had the misguided thought that all of my friends had to be Christians. I was isolating myself in a church fishbowl! I was so culturally separate that I often did not know what people were talking about. In fact, I recall telling one of my friends on the school bus that he should come to church, in response to him asking me to a party. When he asked why, I told him it was either that or hell...the choice was his (that conversation did NOT go well)! Amazingly, he eventually took me up on my offer but only after I shared my story with him. As I read the Gospels, I realized I needed to adopt the mindset of a missionary. I needed to learn to communicate Christ in an understandable way with my potential friends. A missionary often learns a new language and culture to communicate effectively. I started studying my culture, listening to people and learning how they thought. I also began to prayerfully and carefully immerse myself in the culture without giving up my morals. As I read the New Testament, I was encouraged by what I saw in Jesus. He was comfortable interacting with people from a variety of backgrounds and life situations. **His approach was always to love and accept people. He did not lower his standard of righteousness. He was with people where they were and they were attracted to his life.** As I attempted to allow Christ to do this through me, I began to see my friends come to Christ, not in great numbers but one at a time. I discovered that people are much more open to Christ than I had expected. Many people know something is missing in their lives but they just don't know what it is. Unfortunately, many followers of Christ stay away from people with pre-Christian lifestyles. As a result, they are unable to have the impact Jesus said we should have. It is tough to lead people to Christ if you are not their friend!

I want you to think for a minute about your best friend. What is he or she like? (If you don't have a best friend, think for a minute about the characteristics you would like to have in a friend.)

The book of Proverbs describes a good friend as one who has the following characteristics:

- Faithful and consistent (Proverbs 17:17)
- Keeps secrets (Proverbs 11:13, 25:9–10)
- Available and dependable (Proverbs 27:10, 18:24, 20:6, 25:19)
- Has gracious speech (Proverbs 22:11)
- Not easily annoyed but patient (Proverbs 12:16)
- One who understands you (Proverbs 20:5)
- One who helps you become a wiser person (Proverbs 27:17, 13:20)
- Generous (Proverbs 19:6, 11:25, 18:16, 19:6, 22:9)
- Sensitive to your feelings (Proverbs 25:20)
- A friend with your parents (Proverbs 27:10)
- Able to accept advice and a rebuke (Proverbs 13:10, 27:6)
- Pleasant to be around (Proverbs 27:9)

I don't know anyone who doesn't want a friend with the characteristics mentioned above. *Which of these characteristics does your best friend have?*..

Which characteristics would you like to see more of in your life?..

....

What kind of a friend was Levi according to Luke 5?..

What does it tell you about Jesus that Levi was comfortable inviting Jesus to a banquet with his "sinner" friends?..

What do you think it meant that Jesus was a friend of sinners? (Luke 7:34)..

....

How are you purposing to be a friend of sinners?..

....

Friendship is often enjoying something with another person. *What are some things you like to do for fun that you could do with someone who hasn't yet made a commitment to Christ?*..........................

....

Who do you know that needs Jesus that would be interested in joining you in one of those activities?

....

A good friend listens to you. Unfortunately, most of us are not good listeners. We all like to talk about ourselves and our ideas. However, as you are allowing Christ to change you, he is going to show you how to become more others-centered rather than self-centered. You will start to care more about the other person's story rather than the story you want to tell. I encourage you to practice listening to others by doing the following:

- When someone starts sharing something with you, stop and focus on the person. Maintain comfortable eye contact. Face the person if it is appropriate. Let them know by your actions that what they are talking about is important to you.
- Summarize the person's content and feelings. You might say something like, "Let me see if I understand you. Am I correct in saying..." Or, "It sounds like you were stressed at school today." If the response is, "Well, that's really not it," then you didn't hear correctly. Try again!
- Discipline yourself to focus on the person and his or her story rather than thinking about what you are going to say and a story you want to tell.
- Don't interrupt or complete the person's sentences.
- Don't be afraid of a few seconds of silence. Sometimes people need to think before starting to talk again. Be patient.
- Don't be quick to give advice. Listen and care about the person. People are turned off by pushy and arrogant people. Giving a quick answer can feel like both.

Many people are open to Christ when they go through a crisis of some sort. If you have been a good friend before the crisis, your friend will trust you in a crisis. Offer to pray for your friend and be open to sharing Christ especially at that time.

Take a few minutes to ask God to help you be a better friend. Tell God aspects of friendship with which you need him to help you. Ask God to show you someone specific that needs you as a friend.

learn to SPEAK DIRECTLY

MEMORIZE SCRIPTURE ▹

"Then _____ came to _____ and ___, 'All ________ in ______ and on _____ ___
____ _____ to me. _________ go and _____ ________ of all ______, baptizing
____ in the _____ of the ______ and of the ___ and of the ____ _____, and
teaching _____ to ____ everything I have __________ you. And ______ I am
____ you ______, to the ____ end of the ___.'" Matthew 28:__-__

"Then Jesus came to them and said, 'All authority in heaven and on earth has been given to me. Therefore go and make disciples of all nations, baptizing them in the name of the Father and of the Son and of the Holy Spirit, and teaching them to obey everything I have commanded you. And surely I am with you always, to the very end of the age.'" Matthew 28:18–20

Read: Acts 2:1–41; 8:4–8, 26–40

What comes to your mind when you think of the word "evangelist"? Some of us think of televange-lists or street preachers. Millions of people in the United States and around the world have decided to follow Christ because of the gifted ministry of Billy Graham and others who speak directly about the love of God. This is kind of similar to what Peter did on the day of Pentecost. Don't think, however, that the direct approach to sharing Christ has to be done by a trained professional in a stadium. It can be an individual speaking directly about Christ to a person in private like Phillip did with the Ethiopian eunuch. The direct approach works for some because they have not yet accepted Christ and are ready to respond. They just need an opportunity.

Every follower of Christ needs to learn how to share the message of Christ directly. While the direct approach may not be your primary mode, every follower of Jesus needs to be prepared to help people find Christ if they are ready.

The gospel message is simple. Look up each passage of Scripture below and memorize the message. Write them down and put it in your Bible.

- God loves you and has a wonderful plan for your life (1 John 4:16).
- God is holy (1 Peter 1:16) and just (2 Thessalonians 1:6).
- We were created holy but we became sinful (Romans 3:23).
- Because of our sin, we deserve death (Romans 6:23).
- It is only by God's gift of grace that we are able to be saved (Ephesians 2:8–9).
- Jesus who was fully God became a man (John 1:1, 14), died in our place (1 Peter 3:18; 2 Corinthians 5:21), and offers forgiveness as a gift (Romans 6:23).

- You must respond (John 1:12) by asking Christ to be your leader and forgiver (1 John 1:9, 1 Peter 3:15).
- When you do that, the Holy Spirit will transform your life (2 Corinthians 5:17; 1 Corinthians 6:19-20).

Heavenly Father, I pray for boldness to share the message of Christ with people who do not yet know you. I want others to know about you. Help me to be aware of people around me who are open to Christ. Give me the courage to share with them. Give me an opportunity today to talk with someone about who you are and the difference you can make in our lives. Amen.

....

....

....

....

....

NOTES

learn to SERVE PEOPLE

SCRIPTURE ▹

"________ ________ ________ ___ ________ ______ ______, 'All ________ ___ ________ ______ ___ ________ ______

________ ________ ___ _____, ________ ___ ___ ______ ________ ___ ___ ________ ________, ________

______ ___ ______ ________ ___ ______ ________ ______ ___ ______ ______ ___ ______ ______ ________, ______

________ ________ ___ ________ ________ _ ________ ________ ______, ______ ________ _ ______

______ ______ ________, ___ ______ ______ ______ ___ ______ ______.'" ________ ______:___–___

"Then Jesus came to them and said, 'All authority in heaven and on earth has been given to me. Therefore go and make disciples of all nations, baptizing them in the name of the Father and of the Son and of the Holy Spirit, and teaching them to obey everything I have commanded you. And surely I am with you always, to the very end of the age.'" Matthew 28:18–20

Read: John 13:1–17, 34–35; Acts 9

Let me (Claude) share a recent example that profoundly impacted my life. January 1, 2012, my father-in-law David Wessman suddenly and unexpectedly passed away. We mourn his loss while rejoicing in the fact that he is with his Savior; he was a great man of God and an authentic follower of Jesus! In the grief of the days that followed his passing, we were humbled and thankful for the many who sent flowers, meals, letters, texts, e-mails, and phone calls of love and prayers. However, my wife and I were blown away to learn from a text that our friends John and Karen Hart were on their way to babysit our children during the memorial service. What you need to realize is that they drove just under five hours one way, watched our kids for a three-hour window, spent the night at a hotel, and drove the five hours back home the next day. And apart from all that, there were things happening in their lives that made it a difficult, even inconvenient, trip to make. Knowing that our children were being watched by close friends during such a difficult time was huge. It marked my life in a way that makes me emotional even now as I write it. Serving others touches them in deep and real ways!

That's exactly what Jesus did for his disciples and the people around them. When he saw someone in need he served them. The key theme of the Gospel of Mark summarizes this aspect about Jesus: "For even the Son of Man did not come to be served, but to serve, and to give his life as a ransom for many" (Mark 10:45). One of the marks of followers of Christ is their service to others.

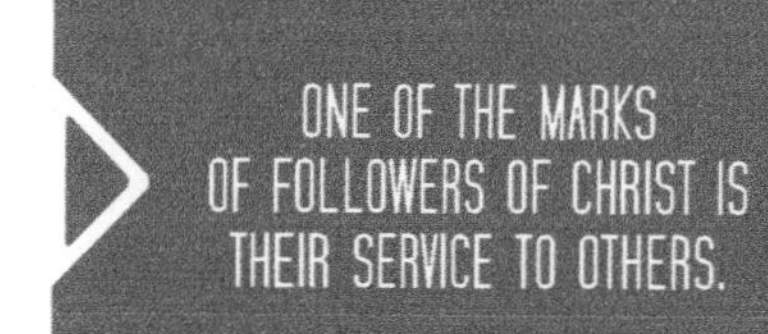
ONE OF THE MARKS
OF FOLLOWERS OF CHRIST IS
THEIR SERVICE TO OTHERS.

One of the most moving stories in the Bible that illustrates this aspect of Jesus is found in John 13:1–17. The disciples and Jesus arrived in Jerusalem for the Passover, a massive Jewish celebration that reminded the Jews how God miraculously brought them out of slavery in Egypt. Jesus and the disciples either borrowed or rented a room where they could have their Passover meal. Normally a servant would be there to wash people's feet as they came into the house, but no servant was there that day. Jesus surprised everyone by taking on the role of a servant and washing all the disciples' feet. Think about it for a minute. The Son of God, the one who spoke the world into existence, the one who would save the world, got down on his knees and washed the dirty feet of his disciples. By doing this, he modeled that no act of service was too low for him or us. John records Jesus teaching his disciples about this in John 13:14–17:

> *Now that I, your Lord and Teacher, have washed your feet, you also should wash one another's feet. I have set you an example that you should do as I have done for you. I tell you the truth, no servant is greater than his master, nor is a messenger greater than the one who sent him. Now that you know these things, you will be blessed if you do them.*

What kinds of things come to your mind when you think about the call to serve people?..................

....

Who around you needs to be served right now? What are their needs?..

....

How can you serve them this week?...

What part of serving will be a challenge for you?...

Talk with your spiritual coach about how to get involved serving in your youth ministry or church. You could also serve your neighbors. You could serve your family. When you serve, you are going to feel God's joy because that's how he designed us. You need to make a decision today to make your life about serving others.

Make that decision now before the Lord.

Jesus, it humbles me that you came to serve people. You are the Creator of the universe. You hold everything in your hand. You have all power and authority and yet you stoop down to wash feet, my dirty feet and my dirty heart. You came to this earth to forgive me of my sin, to show me how to have an abundant life, and to show me how I could be with you forever. Your serving me in those ways humbles me. It brings focus to my life, why I am here. It's not naturally in me to make my life about others. Even when I am serving others, it is often about me, wanting people to affirm me or thank me or appreciate me. I really need your help to learn how to serve in a way that is about you and the people I am serving. Teach me how to do that. Grow a servant's heart in me. Have your way in and through my life. Amen.

learn to MAKE SENSE

SCRIPTURE ▹

"_____ _____ _____ __ _____ ____ _____, '____ ________ __ ______ ____ __ _____ ___

_____ _____ __ ___. ________ __ ___ ______ _______ __ ___ _______, ________

____ __ ___ _____ __ ____ ______ ____ __ ___ ____ ____ __ ____ _____ _____, ____

_______ _____ __ _____ _________ _ _____ ________ ____. _____ _______ _ ___

____ ____ ______, __ ____ ____ ____ __ ____ ____.'" ________ __:__–__

"Then Jesus came to them and said, 'All authority in heaven and on earth has been given to me. Therefore go and make disciples of all nations, baptizing them in the name of the Father and of the Son and of the Holy Spirit, and teaching them to obey everything I have commanded you. And surely I am with you always, to the very end of the age.'" Matthew 28:18–20

Read: Acts 17:16–34

I (Claude) have always had a lot of questions...about everything! In fact, when I was about ten years old I started realizing that my questions made other people uncomfortable. My teachers would act as if I was challenging them, but I sincerely wanted to understand as much as I could. This need for answers spilled over into every area of my life. In my home my questions were received far better. When I had a question about God, my parents would challenge me to find the answer in the Bible (I didn't realize until much later that it was because they didn't have the answer and would find the answer while I was searching). We were following Jesus together, and to this day, I am thankful that they didn't make up an answer or get defensive as a result of my question. In church, well-meaning followers of Jesus would often get defensive when I'd ask questions about God. They took it as a personal challenge of their beliefs. One day an amazing Sunday school teacher by the name of Mike McKeon got down on one knee and asked me to repeat my question...nervously I did. He burst out laughing and said "What a wonderful question! I have no idea what the answer is!" He continued to laugh and insisted that we find the answer together. Honestly, I can't remember for the life of me what that question or the answer was. But it was in that moment I realized that the church was a safe place to ask questions. To this day, as a pastor, I purpose to engage every question with love and openness. Often people will apologize for a question that "may be offensive." I always reassure them that I am following Christ because I have struggled with the same or similar questions and found my answers in him. We should never be defensive when people are trying to make sense out of something that they are planning on surrendering their life to.

Acts 17:16–34 describes the Apostle Paul reasoning in the synagogue with the Jews and God-fearing Greeks and in the marketplace with the philosophers. **The Bible never asks you to shut off your brain. Unfortunately, some are still spreading the lie that you can't ask hard questions and be a follower of Christ.**

How did the Apostle Paul reason with the people from Athens?..

....

What was the result of Paul's reasoning with the philosophers at the Areopagus?..........................

....

Don't miss Acts 17:34, "A few men became followers of Paul and believed. Among them was Dionysius, a member of the Areopagus, also a woman named Damaris, and a number of others."

God used Paul's reasoning ability to draw some to faith in him. Here is what you need to know if you start a conversation with a person who has lots of questions like me:

- Love the person. Don't reject him and attack him because he has questions. Love and acceptance are more powerful than an argument.
- Acknowledge good questions.
- Do not be offended that someone asks a question about a sacred issue. It is not wrong to ask questions about God.
- You do not need to have all the answers. It is much better to say you don't know than to make up an answer. Detailed people notice small inconsistencies, and they enjoy pointing them out.
- Tell the person, "I don't know the answer to that question" when you do not have an answer. Tell him you will try to find an answer for his question and then do it. Part of caring about people is helping them find answers to their questions! While there may not be a definitive answer for

every tough question, there are usually reasonable ones. Some of the authors who wrestle with hard questions are: Lee Strobel, Josh McDowell, C.S. Lewis, and Ravi Zacharias. You could also ask your spiritual coach, youth leader, or pastor for help as well.

- You do not need to have a faith crisis because someone else has a difficult question. Stay close to Jesus. Let others' questions be their questions and yours be yours.
- Pray for your friend. God is the only one who can move a person from non-believing to believing. He often uses circumstances that have nothing to do with an argument to help a person get unstuck.

Don't shy away from those with difficult questions and do not be threatened by them. They are probably seeking real answers, and they certainly need the friendship that you and others offer as the body of Christ. Pray specifically for your friends. Ask God for wisdom to know how to love each one of them, especially those who need God to make sense. It might take a while but if you love them and include them, some will respond to Christ.

Allow your prayer time to be the following: praise God for forgiving you and for welcoming you into his family. Tell the Lord about your friends who need him. Ask God how you can serve them and love them.

Evangelism Styles Questionnaire[1]

Directions

1. Fill in the blanks for all 36 statements according to whether you think the statement applies to you:

3	2	1	0
Very much	Somewhat	Very little	Not at all

2. Transfer your responses to the grid at the bottom of page 144 and total each column.

.... 1. I like to say what's on my mind when I talk to people, without a lot of small talk.

.... 2. I try to learn as much as possible from books and the Internet about controversial issues or important things that are going on in the world.

.... 3. I often use experiences from my own life to illustrate a point I am trying to make.

.... 4. I'm a "people person" who believe that friendship is one of the most important things in life.

.... 5. When I make plans to do something, I really like including new people.

.... 6. I see needs in people's lives that others usually overlook.

.... 7. I don't mind making people feel uncomfortable or putting them on the spot during a conversation, if necessary.

.... 8. I like to analyze things and think through issues.

.... 9. I often identify with others by saying things like, "I've felt that way too."

.... 10. People tell me that it's very easy for me to make new friends.

.... 11. Even if I know the answers, I'm more comfortable having someone who knows more than I do explain Christianity to my friends.

.... 12. Helping other people makes me feel closer to God.

.... 13. I believe in being completely truthful with my friends, even if the truth could hurt the friendship.

.... 14. I like to ask people challenging questions about their beliefs and opinions.

.... 15. When I talk about how I became a Christian, I've found that people are interested in my story.

.... 16. I would rather talk about things that are going on in a person's life than the details of their religious background.

.... 17. If I knew of a good Christian outreach event that my friends could relate to, I'd really work hard to get them to come.

.... 18. I'm better at showing love through my actions than through my words.

.... 19. I believe that if you really love someone, you have to tell that person the truth, even when it's painful.

.... 20. I enjoy talking about controversial issues and debating tough questions.

.... 21. I tell people about the mistakes I've made when I think it will help them avoid those same mistakes and relate to the solutions I've found.

.... 22. I'd rather talk about a person's life before getting into a discussion about their beliefs.

.... 23. I look for Christian concerts and events to invite my friends to.

.... 24. I believe that showing people Christian love through my actions will make them more likely to listen to what I have to say.

.... 25. I believe it's better to risk making a mess of things than it is to do nothing at all.

.... 26. I get frustrated with people who use weak arguments to explain what they believe.

.... 27. People seem interested in hearing stories about things that have happened in my life.

.... 28. I enjoy having long talks with my friends.

.... 29. When I see, hear, or read something I really like, the first thing I think of is other people I know who would enjoy it or get something out of it too.

.... 30. I would prefer doing something practical to help someone rather than getting into a religious discussion with them.

.... 31. I sometimes get into trouble for not being gentle or sensitive in the way I deal with people.

.... 32. I like to find out the deeper reasons why people believe the things they do.

.... 33. Thinking about what God has done in my life really makes me want to tell others about it.

.... 34. People generally think of me as a friendly, sensitive, and caring person.

.... 35. It would be one of the highlights of my week if a friend accepted an invitation to a Christian event.

.... 36. I'm more practical than philosophical—better with actions than ideas.

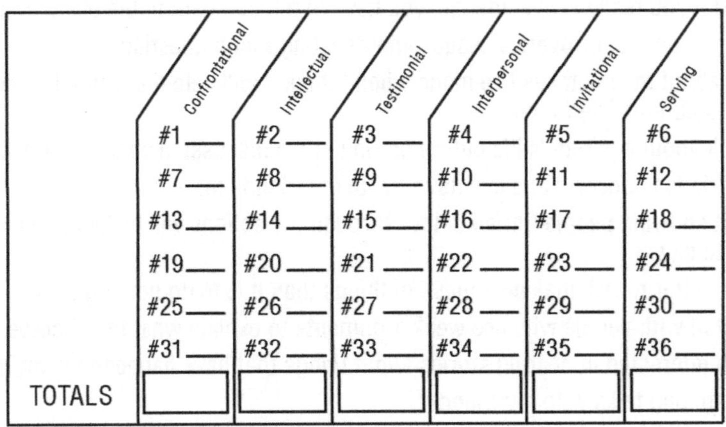

	Confrontational	Intellectual	Testimonial	Interpersonal	Invitational	Serving
	#1 ___	#2 ___	#3 ___	#4 ___	#5 ___	#6 ___
	#7 ___	#8 ___	#9 ___	#10 ___	#11 ___	#12 ___
	#13 ___	#14 ___	#15 ___	#16 ___	#17 ___	#18 ___
	#19 ___	#20 ___	#21 ___	#22 ___	#23 ___	#24 ___
	#25 ___	#26 ___	#27 ___	#28 ___	#29 ___	#30 ___
	#31 ___	#32 ___	#33 ___	#34 ___	#35 ___	#36 ___
TOTALS						

Evangelism Style Examples & Summaries

Confrontational Style—Peter in Acts 2

- Characteristics: confident, assertive, direct
- Cautions: When you confront people with the truth, be sensitive to their feelings. If you push too hard, you might turn them off.

Intellectual Style—Paul in Act 17

- Characteristics: curious; analytical—put a lot of thought into what to say, do, and believe; approach things in a logical way
- Cautions: Don't mistake giving people answers for telling them about Christ. Give reasons and evidence, but remember the goal is to be their friend and look for ways to help them trust Christ, not to win a debate. Be careful of getting into arguments. You don't want to unnecessarily put up walls between yourself and your friend.

Testimonial Style—Blind man in John 9:25

- Characteristics: clear communicator, interesting storyteller, good listener
- Cautions: Make sure you tell your story in a way that relates to other people's lives. In order to do that, you first need to *listen* and then relate your story to their situation.

Interpersonal Style—Matthew in Luke 5:29

- Characteristics: warm personalities, comfortable in conversations, friendship-oriented
- Cautions: Make sure your priorities are straight. Friendships are important, but so is the truth. Sharing Christ with someone challenges their whole direction in life, and that can cause some friction in your relationship. That's a risk we must be willing to take.

Invitational Style—Woman at the well in John 4

- Characteristics: quick to include others in their activities; hospitable; persuasive
- Cautions: Don't let others always do the talking for you. You, too, need to be prepared to share Christ's

love. And don't assume your job is done when people you invite show up at church or a Christian event. Ask them what they thought of the event and look for opportunities to start a spiritual conversation.

Serving Style—Dorcas in Acts 9

- Characteristics: others-centered, humble, patient
- Cautions: Don't let your actions do all of the talking for you. You need to verbally tell people about Christ. Just as words are no substitute for actions, actions are no substitute for words. Don't underestimate the value of your service. Your evangelism style will reach people who might not respond to any other style. Acts of loving service are hard to resist and difficult to argue with—even for the most negative and hard-hearted of people.

QUALITY 4 ▹ DECISIONS, NOTES, PRAYERS...

Relate

What's going on in your life this week?

Review

How is your follow process going?

What memorized Scripture would you like to review?

Reflect

What were the results of your Evangelism Styles Questionnaire?

What are your reactions to the results?

Who is on your prayer list? What has happened as a result of you praying for them?

What did you enjoy most about writing out your story?

What did you think about the discussion concerning the Baptism in the Holy Spirit? Is that something you have experienced? If not, is it something you would like to pursue? If yes, encourage them to draw near to Jesus, to walt for the Holy Spiril lo come upon them, and to yield to the Spirit's promptings.

Refocus

In what ways would you like to grow as a result of what you learned this week?

Resource

What do you need to make that happen?
How can I support you in that?

Prayer

How can I pray for you this week?

Note: Turn to the prayer list you started for this person.
Ask if God has answered their requests from the previous week.
Pray for what they asked and that God would bless them in their next steps as a follower of Christ.

Set and/or confirm the date and time for the next meeting.

....

....

....

....

....

....

PRAYER REQUESTS

QUALITY 5

LEARN TO LOVE

learn to LOVE

Do you have a friend who has that wonderful quality that the more you know them, the more you like them? You might not have recognized it at first, but the longer you hang out with the person, the more you appreciate them. Jesus is like that. The more you get to know him, the more you will love him, appreciate him, and want to be like him! That's partly why we spent two sessions encouraging you to get to know him. The foundation of everything else we are going to learn together flows out of your relationship with him. In one sense you never grow beyond that. It is always about remaining in him and enjoying your loving relationship with Jesus.

Because of what he gives to you, you realize you want to be able to give to him more of yourself out of thankfulness. And, frankly, since life is so much better doing it his way, you don't want to hold anything back from him.

In Quality Two–Learn to Listen, we saw how being with Jesus leads us to people who need healing. Jesus healed and continues to heal people not only of spiritual pain but also of physical and emotional pain as well.

I (Claude) was raised in a Christian home for most of my growing-up years. Being raised in the church, I found myself fearing God and hell; I feared God because I thought he was just waiting for me to screw up to send me to hell! I feared going to hell so much that I responded to salvation in just about every service I was in for about five years (as if that would change anything). I had huge misunderstandings as to what it meant to be in relationship with Jesus. As a result, I had a very legalistic, performance-based perception of Christianity. That, coupled with my desire for approval, led to me being a moralistic church attendee at best. I was good; in fact, I was so good that I was prideful in my good behavior. I had no clue what it really meant to be in relationship with God. I thought everything was about what I had to do, a set of rules to follow, and all the while my Savior was saying "follow me." It wasn't until I was in college (studying to be a pastor) that I thought, "I can't keep this up...being a Christian is too hard!" I still didn't get it and I needed healing.

In a New Testament Survey class my freshman year, the professor (Daniel McNaughton, interestingly enough) said, "Jesus did what we can't do for ourselves." In that moment John 3:16 came to life. The words "can't do" echoed in my heart and mind. The cross was an expression of love where Jesus did everything that needed to be done and he called me to simply follow him, even as he is calling you today. It is our relationship with Jesus that changes us, not our behavior! He loves us. There is nothing that you or I can ever do to make God love us more or less. He loves us because of who we are, not what we do!

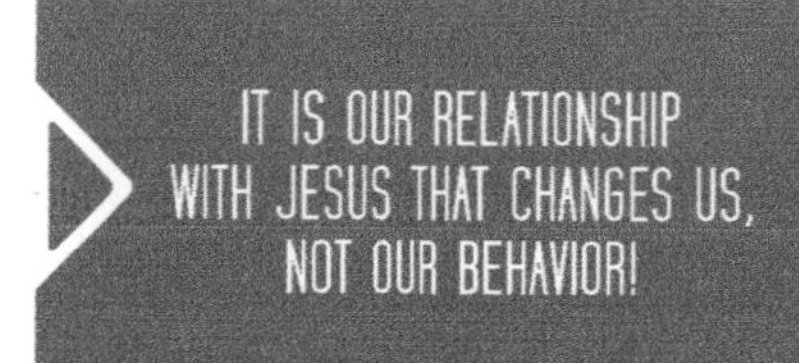
IT IS OUR RELATIONSHIP
WITH JESUS THAT CHANGES US,
NOT OUR BEHAVIOR!

Jesus said, "The thief comes only to steal and kill and destroy; I have come that they may have life, and have it to the full" (John 10:10). The goal for this session is for you to understand the truth about who Jesus says you are so you can enjoy the full life he has planned for you. To do this, we need to do a little probing to see how deeply you believe certain common lies we all struggle with. You will take a brief self-scoring assessment in the first four steps to help you identify where you are with the lies. You will also discover the truth about those lies so you can walk in freedom from now on. Are you ready? Know that I am praying for you as you continue your journey!

God, you have done so much for me in Jesus Christ. Let me discover the truth about who you are and who I am in you so I can walk in freedom before you the rest of my life. Amen.

learn to TRUST GOD

"Jesus replied: 'Love the Lord your God with all your heart and with all your soul and with all your mind.' This is the first and greatest commandment. And the second is like it: 'Love your neighbor as yourself.'" Matthew 22:37-39

◃ MEMORIZE SCRIPTURE

Scripture Memory Review: Matthew 11:28–30; Matthew 7:24–25; Matthew 7:7–8; Matthew 28:18–20

Take the Step 1–Trusting God Assessment on page 176.

Read: Luke 23:32–43

Many people struggle with believing God will forgive them. When we don't realize we can be forgiven, there are only a few options for us. We might *work* to try to get God to like us and to forgive us (volunteer at church, help the poor, give money) in hopes that our good behavior will outweigh our bad behavior. We try to prove to God that we are worthy to be loved. But we always wonder if we did enough so we live under a cloud of fear. We might *ignore* the question of God's forgiveness, trying to not think about it. Since there is nothing we can do about it, why dwell on it? We might *minimize* our sin by saying "everyone does it" or "what I did wasn't as bad as..." We might get *angry at ourselves.* It is a terrible weight to remember what we have done. Some of us beat ourselves up emotionally or in other ways, thinking that if we hurt ourselves enough, maybe we will never do the bad deed again. We might even get *angry at God.* No one is perfect. "Since God is already upset with me for doing wrong, I might as well continue to do whatever I want!" We might do even more destructive things because we've given up on caring what God may think. We might *ask God to forgive* us.

What types of the responses do you see among the criminals crucified beside Jesus?......................

....

What was Jesus' response to the criminal who asked Jesus to remember him?..............................

....

It is really important that you notice Jesus accepted the criminal and that the criminal did nothing to deserve it. Jesus gave him the gift of forgiveness and relationship for eternity simply because he asked.

What is your normal response to dealing with memories of past failures?.......................................

....

My normal response is to work. I (Daniel) tried various ways over the years to prove to God and others that I was worthy to be loved. This was especially true in high school when I was obsessed with becoming a great basketball player. While I loved the game, my real purpose in playing was to prove my worth. I would work out many hours a day to achieve success. I thought if I could achieve certain honors that I would finally feel significant. While I did achieve some success, the feelings of happiness and self-worth were only temporary. I often thought, "There must be more to life than this."

Have you ever felt that way? If so, what did you do to try to find meaning in life?..............................

....

....

One of the problems with thinking this way is that we think our value is established by what we do rather than what Christ has done for us. When we do this, we live our lives based on a lie, that our worth is dependent on us and not God.

Read Romans 5:6–11
Jesus already paid the price for your sin. No matter how hard you work or how perfectly or imperfectly you serve him, he will not love you any more or any less than he does right now.

What are your initial reactions to that statement?

How will knowing this truth affect the way you respond to God?

Thank you, Jesus, for dying on the cross for my sin. It amazes me that you would do that for me. Thank you for making me right before God and for giving me peace and your favor. I am truly grateful. Forgive me for trying to find my worth in something other than you. (You may want to confess some of these things right now if they come to your mind.) I choose to find my worth only in you from this day forward. I rest in you. Amen.

NOTES

learn to SEEK GOD'S APPROVAL

MEMORIZE SCRIPTURE

"Jesus replied: 'Love ____ ____ ____ ____ with all ____ heart and with __ your soul and ____ all your ____.' This is the first and ______ commandment. And the second is ___ it: 'Love your ______ as yourself.'" ______ 22:37–39

"Jesus replied: 'Love the Lord your God with all your heart and with all your soul and with all your mind.' This is the first and greatest commandment. And the second is like it: 'Love your neighbor as yourself.'" Matthew 22:37–39

Take the Step 2–Seeking God Assessment on page 178.

Read: Matthew 9:9–13; Colossians 1:21–22

I (Daniel) am a recovering approval addict. For many years, I believed my self-worth was based on what others thought of me. If I was liked or respected, I felt good. When someone disapproved of me, I felt bad. If someone asked me to do something for them and if it was not clearly sin, I would always try to do it because I wanted them to like me. I was always doing for others, and many people liked me because I helped them. You could always count on me. But inside, however, I wasn't as much of a servant as it seemed on the outside. Many times I resented people asking me to do things for them, but I just couldn't say "no" because I longed for their approval. I was addicted.

I learned this approval addiction lifestyle from my family. My parents were busy in pastoral ministry so they didn't have a lot of time to nurture my brother and me. We received their attention by what we did. If we did something significant, such as get good grades or achieve success in athletics, my parents would praise us. If we did something wrong, we would receive correction. Since I craved positive interaction with my parents, I worked hard to achieve. It created the following cycle in my life: work hard, achieve, receive praise, feel lonely, decide I needed to work harder, repeat. I repeated the cycle hundreds of times.

I applied the same approval pattern to my relationships with others and with God. I joined groups or did things because I wanted the acceptance and approval of others. I tried to be the perfect Christian—reading my Bible every day, praying through long lists every day, going to church events, volunteering for everything—so that God would approve of me. I was working so hard for something Jesus already gave me—his approval. He already approved of me. I just didn't know it.

FINDING YOUR IDENTITY IN
CHRIST WILL SET YOU FREE.

You can see how Jesus thinks about people from the story you read today from Matthew 9:9–13. Matthew was a tax collector. To get that job, he had to team up with the hated Roman government so he could legally steal money from his friends and family. The tax amount was never published, so he could name his own price and pocket the rest after he gave the unpublished but required amount to Rome. People hated the tax collectors because they knew this was happening. But

Jesus looked past all of that and he saw a person whom he loved. While Matthew was still in his sin, Jesus loved him and invited him to follow. Jesus also loved Matthew's friends who were equally in need. That's what Jesus is like! He has always been a friend of people like Matthew, his friends, and anyone else who knows they need forgiveness. He is a friend of sinners like me and you.

When you don't know that, it can really mess you up. If you want God's approval, you may fall into a performance trap. I (Claude) was so relieved to discover that because of what Christ has already done, I am completely accepted by God! Finding your identity in Christ will set you free.

According to Colossians 1:22, what has Jesus done for us?..

....

The word "reconcile" means "to make friendly again, to settle a quarrel." Notice that "reconciled" is a past tense verb.

According to this passage, what event reconciled you to God and what was the result?..................

....

....

It's hard to describe how freeing it has been to discover that I don't have to work anymore to please God. Many people, Christians included, feel unloved, unaccepted, and lonely because they believe the lie that God's love and approval has to do with their behavior.

Just so I make sure you get it, whose behavior makes you approved by God?..................................

You can start your walk with Jesus by knowing the truth that God loves and approves of you because of what Jesus did for you. Because of what Jesus did for you, you are holy, without blemish, and free from accusation. Take a deep breath right now...think about and enjoy God's approval.

Write the following sentence on an index card and repeat it throughout the day: "I am deeply loved, completely forgiven, fully pleasing, totally accepted by God."[1]

How will knowing this truth affect your life?..

....

....

Thank you. I am grateful for your acceptance and approval because of what Christ did for me on the cross. I realize that I don't need to perform to find my value. Help me to accept myself the way you accept me. Teach me to rest in you and enjoy your approval. Allow me to see people the way you do and to accept them the way you accept them, to encourage them to be the individuals you have made them to be. I rest in your approval today. Amen.

NOTES

learn to ENJOY GOD'S ACCEPTANCE

SCRIPTURE

"_____ replied: 'Love ___ ___ ___ ___ with all ___ ___ and with all your ___ and ___ ___ your ___.' This is the ___ and ___ ___. And the second is ___ it: 'Love your ___ as ___.'" Matthew __:37–39

"Jesus replied: 'Love the Lord your God with all your heart and with all your soul and with all your mind.' This is the first and greatest commandment. And the second is like it: 'Love your neighbor as yourself.'" Matthew 22:37–39

Take the Step 3–Enjoying God's Acceptance Assessment on page 180.

Read: Luke 7:36–50

The story in Luke 7:36–50 affects me every time I read it. Although the woman was obviously a "sinner," Jesus received her act of love without embarrassment. He didn't stop there, he gave her salvation and peace! He accepted her, something the Pharisee, at whose home they were eating, could not do. In this story, Jesus makes the point that those who have been forgiven much, love much.

I have met many people who believe those who fail are unworthy of love and deserve to be punished.

They might not say it that bluntly, but their belief shows up in their actions. They feel justified in condemning others who fail, including themselves. They may call others or themselves names, "I am so stupid for..." or, "He's such a loser..." They sometimes make jokes or hurtful remarks about others' failures. They may even make self-deprecating statements about their own shortcomings. They might say harsh words (verbally abuse) or they physically abuse themselves or others. But the bottom line is that someone around them has to pay when failure occurs! The thought behind that belief is this, "Those who fail are unworthy of love and deserve to be punished."[1]

If we are honest, it is hard to deal with ourselves when we fail. None of us is without sin! The truth is that none of us really want justice. I have heard it said, "We want justice for others but grace for ourselves." Romans 3:23 states, "All have sinned and fall short of the glory of God." Some try to convince themselves they don't sin but 1 John 1:8 tells us, "If we claim to be without sin, we deceive ourselves and the truth is not in us." Romans 6:23 tells us the payment for that sin, "For the wages of sin is death." Since we all have sinned and we all deserve death, we all have a problem! If we get justice, we will be separated from God forever. If we don't get justice then God would be a liar. Furthermore, Hebrews 9:22 states, "Without the shedding of blood there is no forgiveness." Someone has to die so we do not have to be separated from our Creator. So we are stuck. Or are we? 1 John 4:10 tells us how Jesus Christ provides the solution for our dilemma.

Summarize 1 John 4:10 in your own words..

....

God sent his Son Jesus to atone for our sins. "Atone" means "to make amends." God sent Jesus to make amends for our sins so we don't receive what we deserve—death and separation from God. It is sobering but it's awesome! God loves you and wants you to have a relationship with him so much that he paid the price for everything you have done that was wrong: past, present, and future! That sets up a new life paradigm for us.

According to 1 John 4:11, what impact will God's atonement have on your relationships?................

....

Based on this passage, how will God's love affect the way you look at yourself when you fail?..........

....

How will it begin to affect the way you treat others when they fail?...

....

What decisions do you need to make in light of these truths?...

....

I (Daniel) learned from Robert McGee in the book *The Search for Significance* that the way out of the failure/punishment pattern is to accept and experience God's love. He suggests focusing many times each day on this thought, "I am deeply loved, completely forgiven, fully pleasing, totally accepted by God, and complete in Christ."[2]

Take the next few minutes right now and think about that statement. Say each phrase slowly and let the truth of God's Word impact your heart and mind. The internal change you experience because of his love will influence every day of the rest of your life!

Thank you, Father, for sending Jesus as my rescuer to pay for my sins completely. I am so grateful that you have accepted me and that I am complete in Christ. Thank you for welcoming me and inviting me to talk with you right now, freely and openly. I am accepted. I belong! Teach me how to extend the same love and acceptance to others that you freely give to me. Amen.

NOTES

learn to PARTNER WITH GOD TO CHANGE YOU

"Jesus _____: 'Love ___ ___ ___ ___ with ___ ___ ___ and with ___ ___ ___ and ___ ___ your ___.' ___ is the ___ and ___ ___. And the ___ is ___ it: '___ your ___ as ___.'" Matthew 22:__-__

SCRIPTURE ◃

"Jesus replied: 'Love the Lord your God with all your heart and with all your soul and with all your mind.' This is the first and greatest commandment. And the second is like it: 'Love your neighbor as yourself.'" Matthew 22:37–39

Take the Step 4–Partnering with God to Change You Assessment on page 182.

Read: John 7:53–8:11; Titus 3:3–7

Have you ever thought, "I am what I am. I cannot change"? Or, "That's the way I've always been, and that's the way I'll always be"? Have you ever turned down an offer to do something you really wanted because you didn't want to embarrass yourself or others if you failed? If so, your sense of who you are and your opinion of your past failures are keeping you from enjoying the life God has for you. Both of the passages you read today provide hope for you. God can change you!

To move out of this kind of thinking and into the new life God has for you, you need a point of view that is based on God's unconditional love and acceptance. Your past failures are a reality, but so is God's unconditional love. To move out of feeling shameful about yourself, you will need to value God's view of you more than your view of your past failures. You know you are struggling with this kind of thinking if you are not pursuing something you really want or need because you are afraid of rejection or failure. The threat of rejection may cause you to withdraw from people and social situations, especially if you are afraid you just won't measure up.

People who struggle with this way of thinking often struggle with a sense of inferiority, habitually destructive behavior, self-pity, passivity, isolation and withdrawal, loss of creativity, codependent relationships, and despising their appearance.[1]

God has a much better way. It is called "regeneration." The moment you began to trust Christ, he made you a new person! 2 Corinthians 5:17 says, "Therefore, if anyone is in Christ, he is a new creation; the old has gone, the new has come!" Everything you and I have ever done was completely forgiven when we trusted Christ. Everything! Because you are no longer held captive by your past and because you are a new person in Christ, you can change. Say out loud, "Because I'm a new person in Christ, I can change. I no longer need to experience the pain of shame."

What did Jesus say to the woman caught in adultery after everyone left?..

....

Notice that while others would condemn her to die, Jesus defended her right to live and then gave her hope that she could start a new life. Jesus does that for you too.

Change may not be easy but it will be worth it. In order to change you need to understand and accept what God's Word says about you.

Summarize Titus 3:3 in your own words...

....

....

According to Titus 3:4–5, what prompted God to save you and how did he do it?..........................

....

....

It is really important that you realize and accept that Jesus saved you not because of righteous things you have done but because of his mercy. Notice that "he saved us" is in the past tense. Jesus did the work to save all of us "by the washing of rebirth and renewal by the Holy Spirit." He washed you and renewed you. You may not always feel like a new person but God's Word tells you the truth about yourself. He gave renewal to you as a gift! God gives you a gift (grace) and your response is gratitude.

According to Romans 12:1–2, what is your part in the renewal process?..

....

What do these verses say should be our response to God's mercy?..

....

What needs to happen so you no longer conform to the pattern of this world?................................

....

What will happen when you do this?...

Talk to God right now about your decision to present your body to him. He sees your heart and he will do the change in you.

Dear Heavenly Father, I am amazed by your kindness and love for me. Thank you for saving me, not because of anything I did but because of your mercy. Thank you for washing my life and for renewing me by your Holy Spirit. I accept this as a gift from you. In view of your mercy, I present my body to you as a living sacrifice. Make me holy and pleasing to you. Renew my mind as well so I can think differently about my life. I want to change. Amen.

learn to ENJOY GOD'S PEACE

SCRIPTURE ▹

_____ _______ ____ ____ ____ ______ ______ ____ ____ ______ ______ ____ ______ ____ ____

____ ____ _______ _____ _______ ______ ____ ____ ______ ______ _____ ________ _________

____ _____ ________ ____ ____ ___ ______ ______ __________ ____ ______ ________ ____ ____ __

"Jesus replied: 'Love the Lord your God with all your heart and with all your soul and with all your mind.' This is the first and greatest commandment. And the second is like it: 'Love your neighbor as yourself.'" Matthew 22:37–39

Review God's Answer for Four Common Lies on page 184.

Read: Philippians 4:4–7

As you study this quality, you may be reframing what you believe about yourself and others by what God says about us. You have explored four lies that can keep you from the best version of life that God offers through Jesus. Today, you will learn how to be free from worry and anxiety. See if you can identify the four commands in Philippians 4:4–7.

This passage teaches us that God can help us learn how to be at peace in all circumstances. The four commands show us how: rejoice (v. 4), be gentle (v. 5), do not be anxious (v. 6), present your requests to God (pray) (v. 6).

Let's be honest. We are not always happy. Painful and difficult things happen that make us sad, confused, or angry.

What kinds of things are you going through right now that are painful or difficult?..........................

....

It is critically important that you understand the difference between being happy and rejoicing in the Lord. Happiness is dependent on your circumstances. For example, I am happy when the weather is nice, but I'm not happy when someone verbally attacks me. You can rejoice in the Lord, however, all the time because he is in control of life's situations. The truth of Romans 8:28 helps me with this, "And we know that in all things God works for the good of those who love him, who have been called according to his purpose." No matter what comes your way, happy or sad, you can always trust God to work things out for the good if you love him. The question you need to ask yourself is, "Do I love God?" If you love him, you can depend on him always! Faithfulness is part of God's character. Your joy is not dependent on your circumstances. It depends on God's character and that never changes. That's why you can rejoice in the Lord always.

Second, when someone hurts you, don't you sometimes want to hurt them back? This passage teaches us that you can always be gentle to everyone. The Greek word for "gentle" means "to show forbearance toward someone." It is what is shown by friends who know one another's idiosyncrasies and weaknesses but like each other anyway. Harshness, on the other hand, can be expected from an enemy. Don't confuse gentleness, however, with weakness. You can be gentle and still do the tough thing. It takes real strength to treat others gently, especially when they deserve otherwise. Never forget, we deserve otherwise! This passage says you can be gentle to everyone because the Lord is near.

In what situations or with whom do you struggle being gentle?..

....

Third, this passage teaches us that we do not ever have to be anxious. Anxiety is worrying about things you can't change. Jesus taught his followers that worrying is worthless. It doesn't change a thing. He said, "Who of you by worrying can add a single hour to his life?" (Matthew 6:27). The assumed answer to that question of course is, "No one." What a waste of time! Corrie ten Boom, a Holocaust survivor said, "Worry does not empty tomorrow of its sorrow, it empties today of its strength." If you put your life in God's hands, you can trust him to take care of you. Change what you have the power to change and leave the rest with God.

What kinds of things are causing you anxiety right now?..

....

Finally, the best way to handle anxious thoughts is to present them to God. That's another way of saying "pray." Talk to God about the things that are on your mind. You can tell him exactly what you are thinking and how you feel. I do a lot of this in my personal journal. Whether you do it in writing or out loud, just pour out your soul to God. Be open and honest with him. Tell him how you feel and what you are thinking. He already knows, but it's emotionally healthy to get it out. God can handle your struggles. He is strong!

The result of rejoicing, being gentle, not being anxious, and presenting your requests to God will be peace, "The peace of God, which transcends all understanding, will guard your hearts and your minds in Christ Jesus." God's peace will guard your mind. You can be joyful, gentle, and free from anxiety at all times and in all circumstances. What an amazing reality. Let the truth of that start to sink into your mind right now.

Take some time right now to talk with God about whatever is on your mind.

QUALITY 5 RESOURCES

Step 1–Trusting God Assessment[1]

Instructions

1. Read each of the following statements and put the appropriate number of the term that best describes you.
2. Add up the total number for each section.
3. Read the interpretation of your score that is found on the next page.

1	2	3	4	5	6	7
Always	Very Often	Often	Sometimes	Seldom	Very Seldom	Never

.... 1. Because of fear, I often avoid participating in certain activities.

.... 2. When I sense that I might experience failure in some important area, I become nervous and anxious.

.... 3. I worry.

.... 4. I have unexplained anxiety.

.... 5. I am a perfectionist.

.... 6. I am compelled to justify my mistakes.

.... 7. There are certain areas in which I feel I *must* succeed.

.... 8. I become depressed when I fail.

.... 9. I am angry with people who interfere with my attempts to succeed, and as a result, make me appear incompetent.

..........10. I am self-critical.

.... TOTAL (See next page for analysis.)

Trusting God versus Fear of Failure

If your score is...

57–70: God has apparently given you a very strong appreciation for His love and unconditional acceptance. You seem to be freed from the fear of failure that plagues most people. (Some people who score this high are either greatly deceived, or have become callous to their emotions as a way to suppress pain.)

47–56: The fear of failure controls your responses rarely, or only in certain situations. Again, the only major exceptions are those who are not honest with themselves.

37–46: When you experience emotional problems, they may relate to a sense of failure or to some form of criticism. Upon reflection, you will probably relate many of your previous decisions to this fear. Many of your future decisions will also be affected by the fear of failure unless you take direct action to overcome it.

27–36: The fear of failure forms a general backdrop to your life. There are probably few days that you are not affected in some way by this fear. Unfortunately, this robs you of the joy and peace your salvation is meant to bring.

0–26: Experiences of failure dominate your memory, and have probably resulted in a great deal of depression. These problems will remain until some definitive action is taken. In other words, this condition will not simply disappear; time alone cannot heal your pain. You need to experience deep healing in your self-concept, in your relationship with God, and in your relationships with others.

Step 2–Seeking God Assessment[2]

Instructions

1. Read each of the following statements and put the appropriate number of the term that best describes you.
2. Add up the total number for each section.
3. Read the interpretation of your score that is found on the next page.

1	2	3	4	5	6	7
Always	Very Often	Often	Sometimes	Seldom	Very Seldom	Never

.... 1. I avoid certain people.

.... 2. When I sense that someone might reject me, I become nervous and anxious.

.... 3. I am uncomfortable around those who are different from me.

.... 4. It bothers me when someone is unfriendly to me.

.... 5. I am basically shy and unsocial.

.... 6. I am critical of others.

.... 7. I find myself trying to impress others.

.... 8. I become depressed when someone criticizes me.

.... 9. I always try to determine what people think of me.

..........10. I don't understand people and what motivates them.

.... TOTAL (See next page for analysis.)

Seeking God's Approval versus Fear of Rejection

If your score is...

57–70: God has apparently given you a very strong appreciation for His love and unconditional acceptance. You seem to be freed from the fear of rejection that plagues most people. (Some people who score this high are either greatly deceived, or have become callous to their emotions as a way to suppress pain.)

47–56: The fear of rejection controls your responses rarely, or only in certain situations. Again, the only major exceptions are those who are not honest with themselves.

37–46: When you experience emotional problems, they may relate to a sense of rejection. Upon reflection, you will probably relate many of your previous decisions to this fear. Many of your future decisions will also be affected by the fear of rejection unless you take direct action to overcome it.

27–36: The fear of rejection forms a general backdrop to your life. There are probably few days that you are not affected in some way by this fear. Unfortunately, this robs you of the joy and peace your salvation is meant to bring.

0–26: Experiences of rejection dominate your memory, and have probably resulted in a great deal of depression. These problems will persist until some definitive action is taken. In other words, this condition will not simply disappear; time alone cannot heal your pain. You need to experience deep healing in your self-concept, in your relationship with God, and in your relationships with others.

Step 3–Enjoying God's Acceptance Assessment[3]

Instructions

1. Read each of the following statements and put the appropriate number of the term that best describes you.
2. Add up the total number for each section.
3. Read the interpretation of your score that is found on the next page.

1	2	3	4	5	6	7
Always	Very Often	Often	Sometimes	Seldom	Very Seldom	Never

.... 1. I fear what God might do to me.

.... 2. After I fail, I worry about God's response.

.... 3. When I see someone in a difficult situation, I wonder what he or she did to deserve it.

.... 4. When something goes wrong, I have a tendency to think that God must be punishing me.

.... 5. I am very hard on myself when I fail.

.... 6. I find myself wanting to blame people when they fail.

.... 7. I get angry with God when someone who is immoral or dishonest prospers.

.... 8. I am compelled to tell others when I see them doing wrong.

.... 9. I tend to focus on the faults and failures of others.

..........10. God seems harsh to me.

.... TOTAL (See next page for analysis.)

Enjoying God's Acceptance versus Fear of Punishment

If your score is...

57–70: God has apparently given you a very strong appreciation for His unconditional love and acceptance. You seem to be freed from the fear of punishment that plagues most people. (Some people who score this high are either greatly deceived, or have become callous to their emotions as a way to suppress pain.)

47–56: The fear of punishment and the compulsion to punish others controls your responses rarely, or only in certain situations. Again, the only major exceptions are those who are not honest with themselves.

37–46: When you experience emotional problems, they may relate to a fear of punishment or to an inner urge to punish others. Upon reflection, you will probably relate many of your previous decisions to this fear. Many of your future decisions will also be affected by the fear of punishment and/or the compulsion to punish others unless you take direct action to overcome these tendencies.

27–36: The fear of punishment forms a general backdrop to your life. There are probably few days that you are not affected in some way by the fear of punishment and the propensity to blame others. Unfortunately, this robs you of the joy and peace your salvation is meant to bring.

0–26: Experiences of punishment dominate your memory, and you probably have suffered a great deal of depression as a result of them. These problems will remain until some definitive plan is followed. In other words, this condition will not simply disappear; time alone cannot heal your pain. You need to experience deep healing in your self-concept, in your relationship with God, and in your relationships with others.

Step 4–Partnering with God to Change You Assessment[4]

Instructions

1. Read each of the following statements and put the appropriate number of the term that best describes you.
2. Add up the total number for each section.
3. Read the interpretation of your score that is found on the next page.

1	2	3	4	5	6	7
Always	Very Often	Often	Sometimes	Seldom	Very Seldom	Never

.... 1. I often think about past failures or experiences of rejection.

.... 2. There are certain things about my past which I cannot recall without experiencing strong, painful emotions (i.e. guilt, shame, anger, fear, etc.).

.... 3. I seem to make the same mistakes over and over again.

.... 4. There are certain aspects of my character that I want to change, but I don't believe I can ever successfully do so.

.... 5. I feel inferior.

.... 6. There are aspects of my appearance that I cannot accept.

.... 7. I am generally disgusted with myself.

.... 8. I feel that certain experiences have basically ruined my life.

.... 9. I perceive of myself as an immoral person.

..........10. I feel that I have lost the opportunity to experience a complete and wonderful life.

.... TOTAL (See next page for analysis.)

Partnering with God for Change versus Fear of Shame

If your score is...

57–70: God has apparently given you a very strong appreciation for His love and unconditional acceptance. You seem to be freed from the shame that plagues most people. (Some people who score this high are either greatly deceived, or have become callous to their emotions as a way to suppress pain.)

47–56: Shame controls your responses rarely, or only in certain situations. Again, the exceptions are those who are not honest with themselves.

37–46: When you experience emotional problems, they may relate to a sense of shame. Upon reflection, you will probably relate many of your previous decisions to feelings of worthlessness. Many of your future decisions will also be affected by low self-esteem unless you take direct action to overcome it.

27–36: Shame forms a generally negative backdrop to your life. There are probably few days that you are not affected in some way by shame. Unfortunately, this robs you of the joy and peace your salvation was meant to bring.

0–26: Experiences of shame dominate your memory, and have probably resulted in a great deal of depression. These problems will persist until some definitive action is taken. In other words, this condition will not simply disappear one day; time alone cannot heal your pain. You need to experience deep healing in your self-concept, in your relationship with God, and in your relationships with others.

The "Common Lies" listed in the left column of the chart below go along with the assessments that you took in the previous pages. The results of the first assessment (Trusting God) connect with the first common lie listed below (The Performance Trap). The second assessment connects to the second lie listed and so on. Find the assessment that you scored the lowest on and look at its corresponding "Lie" below. Follow that from left to right until you see "God's Answer" to the common lie you may believe.

God's Answer for Four Common Lies[5]

Lie	False Beliefs
The Performance Trap	I must meet certain standards in order to feel good about myself.
Approval Addict	I must approved (accepted) by certain others to feel good about myself.
The Blame Game	Those who fail are unworthy of love and deserve to be punished.
Shame	I am what I am. I cannot change. I am hopeless.

Consequences	God's Answer
The fear of failure; perfectionism; driven to succeed; manipulating others to achieve success; withdrawal from risks.	**Justification** Justification means that God has not only forgiven me of my sins, but also has granted me the righteousness of Christ. Because of justification, I bear Christ's righteousness and am, therefore, fully pleasing to the Father (Rom. 5:1).
The fear of rejection; attempting to please others at any cost; overly sensitive to criticism; withdrawing from others to avoid disapproval.	**Reconciliation** Reconciliation means that although I was at one time hostile toward God and alienated from Him, I am now forgiven and have been brought into an intimate relationship with Him. Consequently, I am totally accepted by God (Col. 1:21–22).
The fear of punishment; punishing others; blaming others for personal failure; withdrawal from God and others; driven to avoid failure.	**Propitiation** Propitiation means that Christ satisfied God's wrath by His death on the cross; therefore, I am deeply loved by God (1 John 4:9–11).
Feelings of shame, hopelessness, inferiority; passivity; loss of creativity; isolation; withdrawal from others.	**Regeneration** Regeneration means that I am a new creation in Christ (John 3:3–6).

QUALITY 5 ▹ DECISIONS, NOTES, PRAYERS...

COACH'S SECTION

Relate

What's new in your life this week?

Review

Were you able to pray for people on your influence list this week?

Did anything unusual happen with any of those relationships?

Reflect

On which of the assessments that you took this week were you the lowest?

Did you agree with the summary?

Refocus

What would you like to do as a result of truth you learned in Quality Five?

What are some possible ways of doing that?

Resource

What resources do you have to make that change?

What obstacles do you see in making that change?

Would you like some accountability around that?

What would that look like for you?

Prayer

How can I pray for you this week?

Note: Turn to the prayer list you started for this person.

Ask if God has answered their requests from the previous week.

Pray for what they asked and that God would bless them in their next steps as a follower of Christ.

Set and/or confirm the date and time for the next meeting.

PRAYER REQUESTS

QUALITY 6

LEARN TO PRAY

learn to PRA

Great friends are an awesome gift. Friends are the ones you contact first when you have a rough day or when you have exciting news. You can share your happiest moments and your darkest moments with them without wondering if they will judge you or think less of you. They tell you when you have food on your face and when they think you're out of line. They celebrate with you when you have big moments in your life. You might not see them for days or even weeks, but when you get together, it is like you have never been apart. Great friendship is amazing!

I (Daniel) had that kind of friendship with my sister, Maralyn. Although she was twelve when I was born, she and I developed a unique friendship. You would think the age difference and the difference in our gender wouldn't have allowed it but somehow none of that mattered. When I was growing up, she served as a surrogate mother for me since my true mother often couldn't be there for me because of her bipolar disorder. During the tough teen years, my father allowed me to call my sister when I needed, to talk through what was on my mind. What a gift that was in an era when we paid up to thirty cents a minute! Our phone conversations kept me alive during a very difficult time in life. Those conversations were like water to my soul.

You may have noticed I am writing about my sister in the past tense. On January 4, 2009, Maralyn passed away from ALS (amyotrophic lateral sclerosis, also known as Lou Gehrig's disease). I think you might enjoy reading part of her last blog that was written just seventy-two hours before she died:

> Water is essential to life, and even though food will no longer propel down my throat, I'm still drinking. Amazingly, I don't feel hungry … but I am thirsty, and I'm drinking as much as I possibly can. Without divine intervention, I will get to heaven some time within the month.
>
> These 18 months since my ALS diagnosis have been the worst and best of my life. Worst because of my deteriorating body … best because of my relationship with Christ.
>
> And I'm beginning to see my friendship with Jesus like water when I'm thirsty … so essential to life. He is the real "living water" referred to in John 4:1–26.
>
> I have many lovely friends, but I've never before known a Friend SO close. Every day we have smiled, laughed, and cried together. And he has comforted me. I've asked his opinion, and he has nodded one way or the other. His close friendship has given me many new perspectives on this earthly life that I had never considered before. He's been closer than my skin...
>
> The only thing that makes me sad is realizing that this intimate friendship with him has been available to me all throughout my life, and I never chose it until now. I missed it … big-time! I guess I was always so busy with my lists, projects, plans and events that I was too occupied to be open to such an idea. Oh, I did my devotions, but so often because I knew I "should." That's a different thing. Now I long to be with him, to feel his hug, to hear his voice, to see his smile. It's so different.

> Here's a piece of motherly advice: Don't wait until you have a terminal illness to seek a true friendship with Jesus. He's ready! It takes setting aside some less important things. It takes listening. It takes openness. But it's so worth it! I hope you become literally thirsty for Jesus. Soon I'll be in heaven, and it will be great to see the scenery, gardens and mansions. It will be great to hear the singing and see what's on the banquet tables. BUT! I can tell you, the thing I'm most looking forward to is meeting my Best Friend face-to-face for the very first time. I'm trying to imagine the thrill...[1]

I don't know about you but reading that makes me want to get to know Jesus better. Go ahead and talk with him now.

Jesus, I join your followers who once asked you, "Lord, teach us to pray." I ask that you will teach me like you taught them. I want to draw close to you and to hear your thoughts. I want my life to be the life you want me to live. So teach me. Thank you for the invitation to follow you into a deeper walk with the Father. Amen.

learn to DECIDE NOT TO PRAY BAD PRAYERS

"This, then, is how you should pray: 'Our Father in heaven, hallowed be your name, your kingdom come, your will be done on earth as it is in heaven. Give us today our daily bread. Forgive us our debts, as we also have forgiven our debtors. And lead us not into temptation, but deliver us from the evil one.'" Matthew 6:9–13

◃ MEMORIZE SCRIPTURE

Scripture Memory Review: Matthew 11:28–30; Matthew 7:24–25; Matthew 7:7–8; Matthew 28:18–20; Matthew 22:37–39

Read: Matthew 6:5–8

Prayer is simply talking with and listening to God. I was always told that there is no such thing as a bad question. Is there a such thing as a bad prayer? Well, Jesus teaches the disciples how *not* to pray.

In these verses, what does Jesus say not to do when you pray?..

Jesus made it clear that prayer is not supposed to be something you do to show how "spiritual" you are. When people do that, prayer becomes about them! That is bad prayer! That doesn't mean you should never pray in public, just that it should never be something you do in order to "look holy." No one is holy except Jesus! When you talk with God privately, he will reward you.

Jesus also taught in Matthew 6:7 not to "keep on babbling like pagans, for they think they will be heard because of their many words." Jesus is telling us we can't manipulate God to do something just by mindlessly repeating phrases.

I know I already talked about having a quiet time, but I want to keep it in front of you so it becomes a habit. Getting alone with God is something everyone can do. You may need to get up fifteen minutes earlier in the morning or stay up fifteen minutes later. We make time for things that matter to us. To pray like Jesus, you will need to find a time and a place that you won't be interrupted or distracted. For me (Claude) it needs to be in the morning. I'm not a morning person at all but I find that when I begin my day by talking with my Savior, my day becomes an ongoing conversation. Beyond that, once I begin my day distractions are all too easy to come by!

What time and place works best for you moving forward?..

....

Take time right now to talk with God about your desire to continue to learn to pray.

NOTES

learn the DISCIPLES' PRAYER—PART 1

"This, then, is how you should ____: 'Our ______ in heaven, ________ be your ____, your _______ come, your ___ be done on _____ as it is in _____. Give us today our ____ _____. Forgive us ___ debts, as we also have ______ our debtors. And lead us not into _________, but _____ us from the evil one.'" _______ 6:9–13

"This, then is how you should pray: 'Our Father in heaven, hallowed be your name, your kingdom come, your will be done on earth as it is in heaven. Give us today our daily bread. Forgive us our debts, as we also have forgiven our debtors. And lead us not into temptation, but deliver us from the evil one.'" Matthew 6:9–13

Read: Matthew 6:9–13

When you are learning something new, good instruction is priceless. That's why people take lessons before trying something for the first time. As I (Claude) think about it, there are countless moments that I wish I had taken lessons before attempting something...surfing, repelling, ice skating, skiing, golfing, driving, etc. I had painful and even destructive experiences that could have been avoided if only I had had some form of instruction before attempting! The most painful would probably be water skiing. I had well-meaning family and friends encourage me that I was athletic enough to "figure it out." "Just stand up and lean back," they said. I still remember the nervous moment when the speed boat pulled away and the slack in the rope went out. In an instant my skis were pushing water and my torso was lifting out of the water. For a split second I was what could be misunderstood as in a standing position. That passed quickly! My feet spread too far apart and in a moment of idiocy I lifted my right leg to take a step and regain my balance. Yes, you read that correctly...what was I thinking? My ski caught the water, tore off and on one ski my body lunged forward. Panicking, I gripped the handle tighter (moment of instruction...if you ever find yourself in this situation, LET GO)! I heard my shoulders make a loud pop noise as water rushed over them. Just as the pain in my shoulders was registering I lifted my head out of the water to, well, breathe. Instantly my head was thrown back by the rushing water (again, LET GO)! Filled with fear, I opened my mouth to gasp for air and instantly my mouth and eyelids, yes, eyelids, filled with water. The pressure was more than I could physically handle. Finally, I let go. As I lifted my head out of the water I could hear the hysterical laughter coming from the boat. Turns out you can avoid a lot of pain and actually have fun water skiing if you just get a few lessons; who knew?

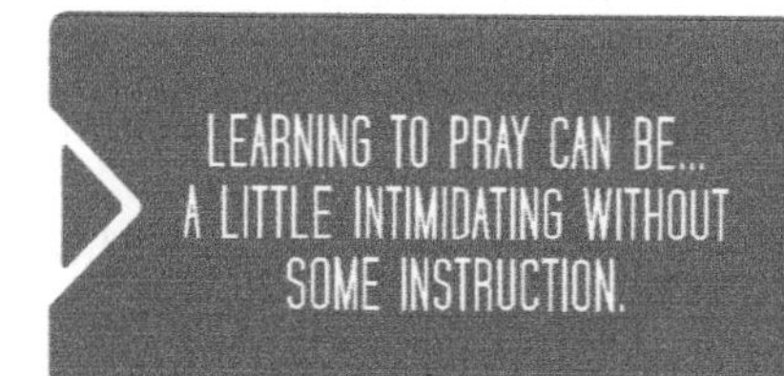
LEARNING TO PRAY CAN BE...
A LITTLE INTIMIDATING WITHOUT
SOME INSTRUCTION.

Learning to pray can be like learning to water ski (minus the pain). It can be awkward, uncomfortable and a little intimidating without some instruction.

In one sense, prayer is easy. It's just talking to God about what's on your mind and then listening to whatever he says to you through his words (the Bible), through your thoughts, or through others.

The first followers of Jesus wanted to learn how to pray so they asked Jesus to teach them (Luke 11:1). If you've read *First Steps: Youth Edition*, you've begun to explore the Lord's Prayer in Quality Six. In the next two steps we are going to unpack that a little so you can learn how to pray with as little pain as possible! Jesus taught his followers six things about prayer. There are three Rs and three Fs. We'll talk about the three Rs today and the three Fs in Step 3.

Relationship ▹ "Our Father in Heaven" teaches us that we are in a loving relationship with our Heavenly Father. Your Heavenly Father loves you so much. He wants you to turn to him and to enjoy his presence. He is inviting you to be with him and enjoys being with you no matter what you're going through, negative or positive. He cares about all your concerns. You may or may not have a good father. But God, your Heavenly Father, will never leave you or abandon you. I know I already mentioned God's compassion in Quality Three–Step 5, but I never get tired of hearing it: "The Lord is compassionate and gracious; slow to anger, abounding in love." Any other view of God needs to be set aside in view of an accurate one.

Take a minute or two right now to thank God for being your Heavenly Father. Tell him that you love him and that you are grateful that he is caring for you. Open your heart to him.

Respect ▸ "Hallowed be your name" teaches us that God is completely pure (holy) and is worthy of our honor and respect. Something pretty cool happens when we start with honoring and respecting God. Resist the temptation to start praying by talking about your needs. We will get to that later, but it shouldn't be the first thing. Tell the Lord how much he means to you and honor him. You may want to kneel right now to show your respect to God. Some people will sing a song or two to God. There are a variety of worship styles. I like songs like "Here I am to Worship,"[1] "How Great is Our God,"[2] "For Who You Are,"[3] "God is Able,"[4] "Our God,"[5] among others. (You can purchase these from iTunes for about one dollar each.) Pour out your love and respect as you sing to God. Don't hold back here. He is worthy of all the honor and glory you and I can give him and more! When you meet with your spiritual coach, ask them if they have some favorite songs or other ways they respect and honor God.

Take time right now to tell the Lord you honor him and respect him. Acknowledge that he is completely pure, that his thoughts and ways are perfect. Honor him with your whole heart.

Reign ▸ "Let your kingdom come" teaches us to start with what God wants. You were not designed to have all the answers for your life. When you pray "let your kingdom come," you are inviting God to be your leader and guide, to rule your life. You lay your life before him and you acknowledge that you belong to God, that you are committed to doing things his way. When you pray "let your kingdom come," you are inviting God to have complete control of your life.

Take time right now to ask God to rule in every area of your life. Talk with God about areas in your life that you have difficulty giving up control: a situation, a relationship, your future. I encourage you to write them down and then share them with your coach.

NOTES

learn the DISCIPLES' PRAYER—PART 2

"This, ____, is ___ you should ___: '___ _____ in _____, _______ be your ____, your _______ _____, your ___ be _____ ___ _____ as it is in _____. ___ __ today our _____ _____. _______ ___ ____ debts, as we also have _______ our ______. _____ ____ ____ ___ _____ _________, but ______ us ____ the ___ one.'" Matthew _:9–13

MEMORIZE SCRIPTURE ◁

"This, then is how you should pray: 'Our Father in heaven, hallowed be your name, your kingdom come, your will be done on earth as it is in heaven. Give us today our daily bread. Forgive us our debts, as we also have forgiven our debtors. And lead us not into temptation, but deliver us from the evil one.'" Matthew 6:9–13

Read: Matthew 6:9–13

In the previous step, we talked about the three Rs of prayer. Try and list them without peeking:

....

Take a few minutes now and pray through the three Rs: Relationship, Respect, and Reign.
If you need to, go ahead and review yesterday.

In this step, we are going to talk about the three Fs.

Food ▸ "Give us today our daily bread" teaches us that we can ask God to meet our most basic needs. When our lives are lined up with his values, we can ask for the strength to do it. You may not be concerned today about whether or not you will have food. Most Americans have that covered pretty well...better than well. I (Claude) really enjoy eating. In fact, I may enjoy it a bit too much! I recently had the amazing opportunity to get away for a couple of days in the Caribbean. As much as I enjoyed getting away I was devastated by the pictures. I'm a typical guy...I rarely weigh myself. After looking at the pictures I realized that I was taking my daily bread two days at a time! Checking online, I discovered that I was about forty pounds overweight for my height and build. Food is good, it's necessary but it had taken the wrong place in my life. Through portion control and discipline not to overeat, I've lost nearly forty pounds! Eating has become less about how I feel and more about food giving me the strength and energy I need to fulfill God's purpose for my life. I've begun what I know will be a lifelong journey of functioning within the range of my daily needs in every area of my life. When our hearts are aligned with God's heart, we can ask the Lord for food to help us. Take a moment right now and ask God to give you the food you need today to do his will for your life. How are you with food? Talk about this with your spiritual coach when you meet.

Forgiveness ▹ "Forgive us our debts as we also have forgiven our debtors" teaches us that when we pray we remember we need forgiveness as much as everyone else. I (Claude) need to remind myself that I live in freedom because God has forgiven me. In turn, how can I justify holding grudges against others? I can't. We can't. Forgiveness is not forgetting, it's not even about trusting someone. Forgiveness is choosing to not make a person pay for what they did. It's letting them off the hook—letting it go. It does not mean you should get back into a similar situation and allow people to hurt you or abuse you again. You may not trust someone because they are not trustworthy, but you can still forgive them. What helped me more than anything was realizing that I deserved punishment for all my sins. God in his mercy paid the price for all my sins, and yours as well, through the death of Jesus Christ on the cross. I don't deserve his forgiveness, but he gives it to me if I will receive it. Complete forgiveness is available to all through Jesus. You can't pay for your sins. Jesus already paid for them! Because he did that for you, you can forgive others. Tremendous freedom is available to you! You don't have to hate anymore.

Freedom ▹ "And lead us not into temptation but deliver us from the evil one" teaches us that God can help you win over every temptation. Most Americans think freedom means being able to do what you want whenever you want. This is not freedom. Proverbs 14:12 states, "There is a way that seems right to a man, but in the end it leads to death." In other words, if you do what you think is right, eventually it will lead to destruction. Real freedom is being able to please God with the way you live, the reason that you were created. With God's help we can be delivered from the things that are destroying us. That's why we need to ask for freedom from temptation and deliverance from the evil one. So we can have the strength to turn towards Christ in everything and keep him the center of our life. If you ask God, he will help you with this.

Let the Lord's Prayer guide you as you talk with God now.

(Relationship) *Thank you, Heavenly Father, for inviting me to be your child. It's incredible to know you welcome me and care for me.*
(Respect) *You are pure and worthy of all praise and honor. There is no one like you. You are amazing. I worship you with everything that I am!*
(Reign) *Lead me in my life today. Have your way in me. Direct and shape me in a way that brings honor to you. I surrender to your complete control of my life. Have your way in my school, relationships, and home. Help me to love those around me like you want them to be loved.*
(Food) *Thank you for providing for my physical needs today, for food, shelter, and clothing. I have everything I need because you provide it. Help me to use every ounce of energy and all my resources for your purposes today.*
(Forgiveness) *Thank you for forgiving all my sins. (Admit to God any specific things you've done recently that you know are wrong.) I accept your complete forgiveness for my sins because of what Jesus did on the cross. Thank you. I forgive (name the person[s] you need to forgive) for (describe to God what the person did that hurt you). Because you forgive me, I can forgive them.*
(Freedom) *Guide me in the right direction today. Give me the strength to stay away from things that are destructive. Deliver me from (name the specific thing that you need freedom from). Thank you for the freedom I have because of the finished work of Jesus Christ. I am a new person today because of what you have done for me. I ask this in Jesus' name, amen!*

learn to PRAY THROUGH PAIN

MEMORIZE SCRIPTURE ▹

"This, ____, is ____ ____ ____ ____: '____ ____ in ____, ____ ____ ____ ____, your ____ ____, your ____ be ____ ____ ____ as ____ ____ ____ ____. ____ ____ ____ our ____ ____. ____ ____ ____ ____, as we also have ____ our ____. And ____ ____ ____ ____ ____, but ____ us ____ the ____ one.'"
Matthew 6:_-__

"This, then is how you should pray: 'Our Father in heaven, hallowed be your name, your kingdom come, your will be done on earth as it is in heaven. Give us today our daily bread. Forgive us our debts, as we also have forgiven our debtors. And lead us not into temptation, but deliver us from the evil one.'" Matthew 6:9–13

Read: Matthew 6:14–15

I (Claude) remember a time as youth pastor when the lack of forgiveness was destroying the students in our group. It was a season of growth for our group but as more and more teenagers began coming in, it was clear that they were hurt in very real and deep ways. They had experienced the forgiveness that Christ makes available but they were being held back in their true freedom because of the lack of forgiveness in their own lives. They were carrying lists of those that had wronged them in their hearts and it was crippling them. I felt lead to do something at the close of a service. I asked everyone to write down the name of someone that hurt them and the offense that they committed. I then told them that if they are willing to forgive this person as Christ has forgiven them, come forward and throw the offense away. At first there was a strange silence but one by one students began coming forward. I'll never forget the first student that came forward...she wanted more pieces of paper! I was amazed at what God did next: they started walking across the room asking for forgiveness from one another face-to-face. Something powerful happened that night: people were set free because they forgave others. I'll be honest, I wrote some things down that night too. It felt great! You only hurt yourself by holding onto the offenses of others.

Write down the persons or incidents you know you need to forgive. Don't wait! Do it now. You'll probably add to your list as you remember things later.

....

....

....

....

....

....

Take one incident at a time to pray through this process:

1. Pour out your soul to God (Psalms 13, 51:17). Tell God about the specific event that caused you pain. Pour it out. Tell him what happened and how you feel about it. Tell God about it until you know you've said everything that needs to be said. Don't censor yourself. He can take it. There is actually a specific kind of psalm that is designed to help you pour out your heart to God when you are in pain. It is a called a "lament" psalm. There are more laments than any other type of psalm.[1] So be encouraged to be open with God about your pain. Tell him or write out what you think about what happened to you. (I, Daniel, find writing is more helpful to me. I can look at it and see it when I am done.) Tell God exactly how you feel. You can tell God your thoughts, pain, and concerns without worrying that he'll be offended or shocked. It's healthy for you emotionally and spiritually to pour out your soul to God.

2. Let God comfort you (2 Corinthians 1:3–4). After you have poured out your heart, invite God into the painful memory. Ask God what he thinks about your painful situation. Listen to your thoughts and impressions at that point. He may remind you of a passage of Scripture. He may give you a new thought, or a comforting picture. It is always different for me. Nothing can separate you from the love of God (Romans 8:39)!

3. Confess your sin (1 John 1:9). What happened to you may have been sad, terrible, or something that was not your fault. However, we all need to take responsibility for what we did afterwards. I hated people and tried to work harder to convince myself that I was worthy to be loved. That was against God's plan for my life. It was sin. You need to confess whatever you did as a result of your situation that was against God's principles. Confessing something is just agreeing with God that what you did was not right.

4. Ask God to restore your soul (Psalm 23:3; 2 Corinthians 5:17). 2 Corinthians 5:17 says, "Therefore, if anyone is in Christ, he is a new creation; the old has gone, the new has come!" Be still and quiet for a few minutes in God's presence, knowing that you are restored to relationship with God.

5. Identify the lie (2 Corinthians 10:4–5; John 8:32). Behind every sinful act is a lie, something you believe about yourself, God, or another that is not true. As you think about the painful incident, what are your thoughts? You may want to write them down. What you told yourself as a result of the painful incident may hurt more than the incident itself. If you can identify the lie, you can replace it with the truth! You may need help from your spiritual coach, a pastor, or a counselor to identify the lie, but it is worth exposing it because the truth will set you free. I will give you an example. Growing up I (Claude) had a teacher say often—and rather definitively—that I "should learn to work with my hands" whenever I would be confused about something. As an adult, I realize that it was a poorly timed and rather cruel attempt at a joke. But as a child I heard, "I was dumb." This lie was surrounded by other situations and struggles that made me begin to believe it was true. This became a personal and secret struggle of my life until God showed me it was a lie. Coauthoring this book in many ways is proof that identifying a lie and replacing it with truth will set you free!

6. Replace the lie with truth (Psalm 1; Philippians 4:4–9). Any and all truth is ultimately found in Christ. However, you may need help to identify the truth about your situation. Talk this through with your spiritual coach. If he or she doesn't know, both of you can ask your small group leader, youth leader, or your pastor. If they can't figure it out, you may want to go to a good Christian counselor. There are several passages of Scripture that helped me replace my lie with the truth. Psalm 139:13–16 was powerful for me:

> *For you created my inmost being; you knit me together in my mother's womb. I praise you because I am fearfully and wonderfully made; your works are wonderful, I know that full well. My frame was not hidden from you when I was made in the secret place. When I was woven together in the depths of the earth, your eyes saw my unformed body. All the days ordained for me were written in your book before one of them came to be.*

According to God's Word, I was not a mistake. God thought about every day of my life before I was born. When I start to feel insecure or insignificant, I can tell myself the truth. God loves me. I'm here for a purpose. He knows everything about me and he has my life in his hands. I am secure in him. That truth changed my life.

Who or what are the people or situations that you need to pray through? Your caring Creator can set you free through the process you have learned today. He used it to change my life. It may take months for you to get through your list but when you are done you will feel like a new person! And you will never want to go back to the old way. When you come to Jesus, you find rest for your soul. Take one incident or a person on your list and walk through the process right now. Freedom is just around the corner!

learn to DO SPIRITUAL WARFARE

“This, then is how you should pray: ‘Our Father in heaven, hallowed be your name, your kingdom come, your will be done on earth as it is in heaven. Give us today our daily bread. Forgive us our debts, as we also have forgiven our debtors. And lead us not into temptation, but deliver us from the evil one.’” Matthew 6:9–13

Read: Ephesians 6:10–20

The Bible teaches there is more to this world than what you see. There is a real devil. There are rulers, authorities, and dark powers in this world and spiritual forces of evil in the heavenly realms (Ephesians 6:12). I wish it wasn’t true, but it is. Their sole purpose is to fight against the work of God and to destroy your life. The evil one and his forces fight dirty. They rarely attack head on. When you are tired, hungry, or lonely, they move in to try to mess up your life! Ephesians 6:10–20 shows you how to fight and win against these destructive forces. There are eight commands in this passage that show you how to win.

Read Ephesians 6:10 again. What are we commanded to do?..

....

It is absolutely essential to know where your strength comes from. Notice it doesn't come from within you. It is the American way to try to be independent. Some of us won't ask for help unless we absolutely have to. If that is you, you're going to have to make a decision to find your strength in God and not in yourself. None of us are strong enough on our own to fight against the unseen forces of darkness. You will always win though if God is your source of strength. No one is more powerful than God. It is his power that raised Christ from the dead. It's the power of God that brought the world into existence. It is his power and his alone that is changing your life. When you tap into his power, you can't lose. Who's strength will you depend on, the Lord's or your own?

What are some ways that you currently depend on yourself rather than God?..................................

....

The rest of today's guide will help you learn to fight in the spiritual realm. Ephesians 6:11 is a summary statement for how to fight and win. First, you must "Put on the full armor of God." You can't afford to only put on part of the armor of God. You need the full armor of God. You are vulnerable if part of you is missing the proper armor.

My (Daniel's) nephew, David Mathias, was a surgeon in the Army during the early part of the war against Iraq. He was one of the surgeons on duty on "Black Sunday." Minutes after taking over operations, the First Cavalry Division was ambushed in Sadr City. The twenty-four hour firefight left eight Americans dead and over sixty wounded. What struck me about the story was not that young men and women died in war. That's a reality of war. What upset me the most was that many of our troops were wounded and died because they did not have proper armor.[1]

You can be fully protected in spiritual battles! Notice that the word "stand" repeats in Ephesians 6:11, 13 (two times), 14. You can take your stand, resist the attacks of the evil one and not be shaken when you do spiritual warfare, if you put on the full armor of God. You need it all!

Armor Piece #1 ▹ The Helmet of Salvation. Accepting the finished work of Christ for you on the cross protects you from fatal head wounds. Take a moment to thank God that he saved you by dying on the cross for your sins. Don't try to work for it, just accept it and thank God.

Armor Piece #2 ▹ The Sword of the Spirit which is the Word of God. The only offensive weapon you have is the Scriptures. Over the next months and years, as you dig into the Scriptures, you will discover how powerful the Word of God is.

Armor Piece #3 ▹ The Belt of Truth. When you know the truth found in the Scriptures, you are no longer vulnerable to the lies of Satan. One of the best questions you can ask yourself when you are tempted is, "What lie am I believing?" When you discover the lie and replace it with the truth expressed in Scripture, you win a battle. I find it fascinating that truth is linked to the middle part of our bodies, the sexual part of our bodies. The truth will affect every area of our lives, especially our sexual behaviors.

Armor Piece #4 ▹ The Breastplate of Righteousness. Righteousness is a gift from God that comes by faith in Jesus Christ and it will guard your heart. 2 Corinthians 5:21 states, "God made him who had no sin to be sin for us, so that in him we might become the righteousness of God." Romans 3:22 states, "This righteousness from God comes through faith in Jesus Christ to all who believe." When you trust God to give you righteousness through Jesus, it keeps you from doing things to prove you are righteous. In spiritual warfare, the evil one might bring up your past and tell you how bad or unworthy you are. That is when you remind your enemy and yourself that you are righteous, not because of anything you have done but by faith in Jesus Christ! He makes you righteous. It is a gift, not something you earn.

Armor Piece #5 ▹ The Gospel of Peace. Romans 5:1 states, "Therefore, since we have been justified through faith, we have peace with God through our Lord Jesus Christ." You don't need to fear the attack of the evil one during spiritual warfare because God's peace is with you. There is a reason that peace is linked to your feet. God's peace is active! You must be prepared to bring God's peace to people who are as lost as you once were.

Armor Piece #6 ▹ The Shield of Faith. A shield is a defensive weapon that keeps you safe from arrows that are sent your way. The evil one does not know your thoughts, but he does know how you acted in past situations. He is a student of your destruction. He will send fiery darts your way in the form of thoughts and opportunities to sin to see if you will accept them and then act on them: hateful thoughts, doubts, a burning desire to sin, a reminder of past hurts, etc. When those moments come, your faith in God will keep you from being destroyed. When you are tempted, by faith decide to act on what God's Word says and he will keep you safe!

Armor Piece #7 ▹ Praying in the Spirit. Notice how many times prayer is mentioned in Ephesians 6:18–20, "And *pray* in the Spirit on all occasions with all kinds of *prayers* and *requests*. With this in mind, be alert and always keep on *praying* for all the saints. *Pray* also for me, that whenever I open my mouth, words may be given me so that I will fearlessly make known the mystery of the gospel, for which I am an ambassador in chains. *Pray* that I may declare it fearlessly, as I should" (emphasis mine). One of the powerful weapons you have in spiritual battle is prayer, talking with God. There are many different kinds of prayer available to you. Use them all. Praying in the Spirit is praying beyond your mind and words. Have you ever prayed for a while and run out of words, but you feel like you are not done praying? That's the feeling I get right before I pray in tongues. There are many references in the Bible to people being empowered to pray in a heavenly language they never learned (Acts 2:4, 10:44–45, 19:6; 1 Corinthians 12:10, 12:30, 13:1, 14:1–25). The wonderful thing about praying in the Spirit is that the Spirit of God prays through you. Where your words are inadequate, the Holy Spirit can give you words in a heavenly language that adequately express to God what needs to be said. When we pray powerful prayers, powerful things happen. I believe the Bible teaches this experience is available to all believers for private prayer. Some people will use this in public prayer as well, but then there needs to be an interpretation. If you have never heard of this before, you may want to talk about this with your spiritual coach.

Protector, thank you for giving me the armor and the weapons I need to win in spiritual battle. Teach me how to use each piece of armor and the weapons of spiritual warfare. Thank you for winning the war against sin and death through the cross. Enable me to win in battle against the spiritual forces of evil in the heavenly realms. Empower me to pray in the Spirit so I can pray more effectively. I need and want all you have for me. I want to be fully prepared for spiritual battle. Amen.

....

....

....

....

....

NOTES

QUALITY 6 ▹ DECISIONS, NOTES, PRAYERS...

COACH'S SECTION

Relate

What was the highlight of your week?

Review

How did it go with your thought process this week? (loving God, identifying any lies, replacing the lies with the truth)

What progress have you made?

Reflect

What stood out to you as you worked through this quality?

On Step 2, there was a discussion about areas that we have difficulty giving up control. Did you have any areas you would like to discuss?

On Step 3, there was a discussion about food. How are you with food?

What did you think about the process for "Praying Through Pain" on Step 4? Do you have any areas you prayed through or would like to pray through that you want to talk about?

How clear was it to identify the lie?

On Step 5, there was a discussion about "praying in the Spirit." What experience do you have with praying in a prayer language?

Refocus

What would you like to do as a result of what you read and learned this week?

Resource

What do you need in order to make that happen?

Prayer

How can I pray for you this week?

Note: Turn to the prayer list you started for this person.

Ask if God has answered their requests from the previous week.

Pray for what they asked and that God would bless them in their next steps as a follower of Christ.

Set and/or confirm the date and time for the next meeting.

....

....

....

....

....

....

PRAYER REQUESTS

QUALITY 7

LEARN TO MANAGE

learn to MANAG

Read: Deuteronomy 6:4–5

I (Claude) was always rather good at certain things. You know what I mean, you have them too. Things that just come natural to you. Well, as a result of being good at certain things, I put very little effort towards them. I had the thought that if it came naturally to me then I should lean back and enjoy the fact that I didn't have to try very hard. It never occurred to me that I had certain strengths that I should develop. Instead, I sat on my strengths and complained about my weaknesses. It wasn't until I had an art teacher tell me that it was a "waste" to have such a gifted person doing the bare minimum. Waste? I thought about that statement for days. In what other areas was I wasting the way God had wired me? As I began thinking about what God was leading me to do with my life "when I grew up," I started to fear that I was wasting my one and only life! I wanted to honor God with my life, not just get by. I began to apply myself in several different areas but to stick with my example, I began to excel in my artwork. My God-centered efforts led to not only being voted "most artistic" by my senior class (how many pastors can say that, ha) but more importantly earned me scholarships at college that ultimately led to me being able to pursue my call to ministry! I was also able to sell artwork while at college to pay bills. I'm glad that I realized what I was risking by not managing the gifts God had given me. My whole life and all my gifts are an opportunity to worship God! I want to honor him in everything I do. Loving God involves every area of your life: time, energy, money, influence. Everything. Beyond that, God expects a return on his investment in our lives. God put you and everyone else on the planet, during this time in history, because he wants and expects each one of us to fulfill a specific purpose for the advancement of his kingdom. Wrapping your head around that will change every decision you make for the rest of your life.

As you take each step, you will look at a different aspect of your life and how to worship God in that area of your life: mind, money, body, speech, time. Remember to focus on loving God as you develop healthy habits. Don't get discouraged as you start to work in these areas. Developing these venues for loving God is a Christ-centered process. This step is just a start.

Thank you so much for loving me. Your kindness is amazing. You have forgiven me of my sins, the things that separated me from you. I am truly grateful. You have given me a hope and a future when I had nothing. As I look at my resources and how I can love you in everything, I ask you to continue to make me aware of your unending love. Help me to establish good habits as an expression of that love. Lord, you have given me so much. I want to use it to bring honor to you. In your name I pray, amen.

learn to MANAGE YOUR MIND

"But seek first his kingdom and his righteousness, and all these things will be given to you as well." Matthew 6:33

Scripture Memory Review: Matthew 11:28–30; Matthew 7:24–25; Matthew 7:7–8; Matthew 28:18–20; Matthew 22:37–39; Matthew 6:9–13

Read: Philippians 4:8

We already talked about the verses right before these, Philippians 4:4–7, on Quality Five–Step 5: how God gives you peace of mind when you rejoice in him always, are gentle to everyone, choose not to be anxious about anything, and pray about everything.

What is the one command in Philippians 4:8?..

The Greek word for "think" doesn't simply mean to "think" by trying to ignore other thoughts. It means "to reckon, evaluate, to consider, ponder, let your mind dwell on."[1] What you think about, you will become. What you dwell on is extremely important to your walk with Christ. Put simply, the Apostle Paul is not teaching his readers through this passage to only think about Christian books, movies, and music. He is teaching them (and us) to filter what is around you from a Christian perspective. You do this by intentional thinking. 2 Corinthians 10:4–5 reads:

> *The weapons we fight with are not the weapons of the world. On the contrary, they have divine power to demolish strongholds. We demolish arguments and every pretension that sets itself up against the knowledge of God, and we take captive every thought to make it obedient to Christ.*

To take your thoughts "captive" you need to notice what you are thinking, and then ask yourself if that thought helps you become obedient to God and his plan for your life. If the thought doesn't, you must reject it and replace it with the truth as defined by Scripture.

I like Philippians 4:8–9 because it gives a summary about how a spiritually healthy mind thinks. There are things we need to think about.

What are they?..

What is truth? What's true to you might not be true for someone else, right? Well, Christ-centered thought clears up that question. Jesus said, "I am the way and the truth and the life" (John 14:6). In other words, Jesus said truth is a person. If you want to know what truth is, you can't look within yourself. Proverbs 14:12 states, "There is a way that seems right to a man, but in the end it leads to death." Similarly, Jeremiah 17:9 states, "The heart is deceitful above all things and beyond cure. Who can understand it?" Jesus also said in John 17:17, "Sanctify them (the disciples) by the truth; your word is truth." Truth then is God's perspective as shown in Jesus and in God's Word.

People who work with money can identify counterfeit money quickly because they work with real money all day long. You'll be able to identify what truth is by spending time with Jesus and in his Word.

What does God say about you or your life that you have a hard time believing?...............................

....

....

(Share your answer with your spiritual coach so you can have his or her perspective.)

What comes to mind when you think "noble"?...

....

Noble means "honorable, worthy of respect, above reproach." If you are going to think about noble things, you may want to make some decisions about the kinds of movies or television shows you watch. I am not saying that you should put your head in the sand and avoid what is unpleasant and displeasing. But if you know that the general purpose of a movie or show is not "above reproach," you don't want to willfully expose yourself to it. There are better things to think about!

What do you currently watch that needs to change?..

....

The Bible defines "right" as something that falls in line with the laws of God and living according to that. In other words, it is right if God says it is right.

How does this understanding of "right" affect how you think about something?...............................

....

Purity refers to moral purity. You must realize that between media and personal relationships, you will be bombarded with sexual promiscuity in our culture. That being said, how and why would you choose to be morally pure? First let me say, sexuality is not wrong. God created us as sexual beings. As a teenager, you must guard yourself against settling for a ripped-off version of what God wonderfully provides in the marriage relationship. That begins in the battlefield of the mind! If you want to be loved, know you are loved by God. If you want to belong, know that you belong to Christ. If you want to simply feel good, know that lust is an idol that never fills that void. What you are truly wanting is the joy that's only available in following Jesus! It is not pure to lust after a two-dimensional image on a computer or to fantasize about the latest "hot" musician. However, it's not the point to just stop doing or thinking bad things. You can try to manage your mind with a "be a better person" motivation. **Following Jesus is not behavior modification, it's identity modification.**

Your relationship with Jesus will begin to show you the idols in your life that you need to stop serving...and that will set you free! Freed people have different behavior and think differently simply because they are free.

What idols of impurity are you serving?..

What do you need to know about God to set you free?..

....

What kinds of things do you need to start thinking about that are pure?..

....

Lovely things are "cheerful, pleasing, and agreeable." They are beautiful. Music, nature, art, athletics can all be "lovely." When you filter life through what is lovely from God's perspective, you find beauty and then thank God for it.

What are some ways that you personally can focus on what is truly lovely?..

....

....

"Excellent" carries with it a sense of quality that includes virtue, morality, and integrity.

"Praiseworthy" means action worth talking about that shows God's moral character.

Read Philippians 4:9. *What will happen if you think about these things and model your life after godly people?*..

....

There is nothing like having God's peace with you!

What changes do you need to make with your thought life?..

....

What can you do to be more intentional about your thought life moving forward?..............................

....

(Thank God for the freedom he offers you to learn how to think his thoughts. Tell God specifically how you intend to make changes in your thought life as a result of knowing him. Ask God to help you learn how to think in a way that honors him and brings you the peace and joy you are looking for.)

Final thoughts:

I heard this summary about the impact of our thoughts:

Sow a thought, reap an action.
Sow an action, reap a habit.
Sow a habit, reap a character.
Sow a character, reap a destiny![2]

Proverbs 4:23 NCV, "Be careful what you think, because your thoughts run your life."

NOTES

learn to MANAGE YOUR MONEY

MEMORIZE SCRIPTURE ▹

"But seek ____ his kingdom and ___ righteousness, and ___ these things will be _____ to you as ____." Matthew 6:33

"But seek first his kingdom and his righteousness, and all these things will be given to you as well." Matthew 6:33

Read: Matthew 6:14–15

I (Claude) grew up in a middle-class family. We always had food on the table, a place to sleep, clothes to wear and a roof over our heads. I didn't always have the nicest things, and at the time, I thought that mattered. I wanted to fit in and in my world that meant wearing certain clothes, sneakers, and the list goes on. I know you know the tension I'm talking about. No matter how much you have, someone has more! I was almost a slave to my desire for things until...until the day that all changed. I came home from school and found out that my dad had gotten a second job working nights at Burger King so that we could make ends meet. Most teens would be embarrassed of that in my suburb, but honestly, it never occurred to me. I was proud. Even now I am emotional. My father was teaching me about hard work, providing, and priorities. Our home was a place of love; stuff didn't matter. I watched as my parents went without so we could have Christmas presents. Suddenly

I didn't care that beans and rice were for dinner again. I saw my parents faithfully continue to tithe (give ten percent to the church) every week when they could have justified keeping more money for themselves. That year I learned that you are defined by who you are, not what you look like or what you do. When you learn that your worth is found in Christ, money takes its rightful place in your life.

Jesus addresses this area of your life in Matthew 6:19–33. *First Steps: Youth Edition* discusses Jesus' warning against storing up for yourself treasures on earth.[1] Your heart will go where you put your treasure. Beyond that, Jesus reveals the fact that we can't serve both God and money (Matthew 6:24).

At this point in your life, would you say that you are serving money? If so, what impact does it have on your life?..

What change(s) would you like to make in this area of your life?..

....

In Matthew 6:25–32, Jesus talks about why worrying is worthless. What are some reasons Jesus gives for why that is?..

In Matthew 6:33, what does Jesus tell you to do instead of worrying?..

....

What decision(s) would you like to make based on the change(s) you listed above and the truths described in Matthew 6:19–33?..

I could tell you many stories of God's provision but those are my stories. You need your own stories about what God has done because you surrendered your money to him. You and the Lord can write a new story together of God's faithfulness and miraculous provision. You will never know what that story would have been if you don't surrender. Stories of need can be replaced with stories of generosity...God's grace-filled generosity to you, and in turn, your joyful generosity to others. God is amazing. Trust him! Make the decision to follow him with your finances and don't look back. You may not have a source of income right now but that doesn't have to stop you from making the decision to keep money in its proper place in your life, for the rest of your life! I've never regretted the decision I made to surrender my finances to God. God has blessed me in so many ways because of that. I want that for you, and I know he does too!

If you do currently have a job and would like to know how to take the next practical steps with your finances, there are several places you can go to find great resources.[2] You can also talk with your spiritual coach about this. He or she may have some suggestions for the next steps about how to put God first in your finances.

My Provider, I love you. You have forgiven me of my sins and given me a new life in Christ. You do all things well. I trust you. I make the decision today to surrender my finances to you. I choose not to serve money any longer. I'm still figuring out all that that means but I trust you. Have your way in my finances. Amen.

learn to MANAGE YOUR BODY

"But ____ ____ his ______ and ___ ____________, and __ these things ___ ___ _____ to you as ____." Matthew _:33

"But seek first his kingdom and his righteousness, and all these things will be given to you as well." Matthew 6:33

Read: Deuteronomy 6:5; Genesis 1:26–31

Genesis 1:26–31 can help you realign your life and how you view your body. There are three things you must understand from these verses. First, God created you. You are not self-made. You didn't evolve over a long period of time from an earlier life form. There is a personal, Creator God who designed you. You are different from anyone who has ever been on this earth. Second, you are made in God's image. This means you are uniquely designed to partner with God as his representative in your world for this time in history. You were not designed to do your own thing. You have a purpose! To get the third point, you need to reread Genesis 1:31.

What did God think about the humans he had made on the sixth day?..

If you look back over Genesis 1 at the end of the other five days, you will see that God said, "It was good." It was only after he made humans that God said, "It was *very* good" (emphasis mine). When God looks at you, he sees a masterpiece. The media have taught us to compare ourselves to others and to devalue certain aspects of our bodies that are not like someone else's. That's not God's perspective. He made each person different and special. If you are going to become who God has designed you to be, you have to accept his thoughts about you as truth! Your body is "very good." You will find great freedom when you look at your body and your life from God's point of view. Take a moment right now and read these verses a couple of times and believe it. Psalm 139:13–16:

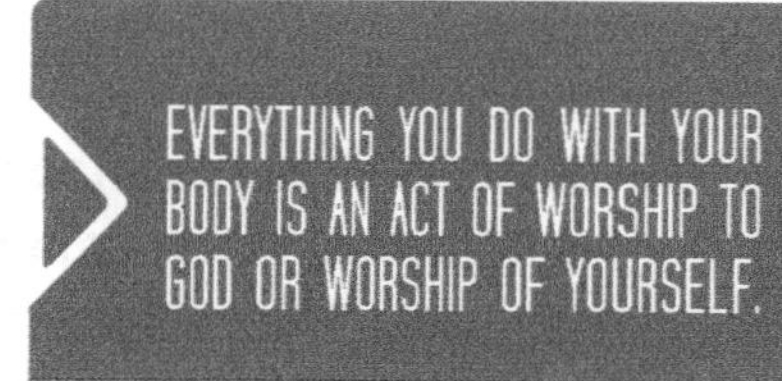
EVERYTHING YOU DO WITH YOUR BODY IS AN ACT OF WORSHIP TO GOD OR WORSHIP OF YOURSELF.

> *For you (God) created my inmost being; you knit me together in my mother's womb. I praise you because I am fearfully and wonderfully made; Your works are wonderful, I know that full well. My frame was not hidden from you when I was made in the secret place. When I was woven together in the depths of the earth, your eyes saw my unformed body. All the days ordained for me were written in your book before one of them came to be.*

Thanking God for your body and accepting his view of it is a huge part of following Jesus. It is also essential that you accept his purpose for your body, to partner with God for his purpose.

Several Scriptures will help shape how you think about your body. First, Deuteronomy 6:5 describes what you do with your body as worship: "Love the Lord your God with all your heart and with all your soul and with all your strength." Worship is not just what you do on Sunday during a service. Everything you do with your body is an act of worship to God or worship of yourself. In practical terms, what you eat, how much or how little you eat, how much you sleep, what you drink, how you work, and how you are in relationships are all matters of worship, ways of expressing your love to God. In the same way, those things can be indicators of who or what you are worshipping instead of God! If you view your body as an instrument to please yourself, you will do your own thing, what feels good or seems right to you. Knowing that your body is a gift from God that you are responsible to take care of should cause you to stop and think about how you can worship and honor him with it. Romans 12:1 describes it this way: "Therefore, I urge you, brothers, in view of God's mercy, to offer your bodies as living sacrifices, holy and pleasing to God–this is your spiritual act of worship." Embracing this view of your body will change everything.

What comes to your mind right now that you will need to change based on the truth of this principle?

....

....

Sometimes when it comes to these kinds of things, people feel like they are going to miss out on a lot of fun. Without a doubt there will be short-term, temporary pleasures you will bypass if you offer your body to God. While temporary pleasures like overeating, drinking, and having sex outside of marriage seem to be fun, in the end they produce much pain and disappointment. Overeating results in all kinds of health problems. Alcoholism and drug abuse destroy bodies and families, and they steal valuable resources that could be used to invest in the future. Sex outside of marriage is always destructive. 1 Corinthians 6:18–20 describes it this way:

> *Flee sexual immorality. All other sins a man commits are outside his body, but he who sins sexually sins against his own body. Do you not know that your body is a temple of the Holy Spirit, who is in you, whom you have received from God? You are not your own; you were bought at a price. Therefore honor God with your body.*

God's ways are always best. After all, he created our bodies! Romans 6:12–13 describes the choice you have with your body now that you know the Lord:

> *Therefore do not let sin reign in your mortal body so that you obey its evil desires. Do not offer the parts of your body to sin, as instruments of wickedness, but rather offer yourselves to God, as those who have been brought from death to life; and offer the parts of your body to him as instruments of righteousness.*

Adjusting what you do with your body is a process. Most people have to start in one area and then move to another.

What aspects of what you do with your body need adjustment?..

....

....

....

(You will want to prioritize these and strategize with your spiritual coach about your next decisions.)

Heavenly Father, thank you for my body. I praise you because I am fearfully and wonderfully made. I haven't thought that way about my body until now. Thank you for accepting me and loving me just like I am. Thank you for showing me how much you value my body; you bought me with a precious price. I accept as truth that my body is "very good." I offer my body back to you as a form of worship. May what I do with my body honor you from this day forward. I need your help as I learn how to do that. Amen.

NOTES

learn to MANAGE YOUR WORDS

"But ____ first ___ ______ and ___ __________, and ___ ______ ______ ___ ___ _____ to ___ as ___." Matthew 6:__

MEMORIZE SCRIPTURE ◃

"But seek first his kingdom and his righteousness, and all these things will be given to you as well." Matthew 6:33

Read: James 3:3–12; Matthew 12:33–37; Ephesians 4:29–32

I (Claude) wonder who came up with the lie, "Sticks and stones may break my bones but words can never hurt me." They must not have known some of the quick-witted, hurtful people I knew growing up! Words hurt. They're powerful and we all know it.

What does James compare a tongue to in order to describe its power?..

....

Powerful communication can serve as a rudder to motivate a large group of people to go in a certain direction. It can also destroy lots of people like a spark can destroy a forest. Words are powerful. As a follower of Jesus, your words must become those which turn people toward Christ. You may have struggled with your words up till now. If you're like me you've said hurtful things to others or even to yourself. Maybe you gossiped about someone or told a story in a way that made someone look bad. I know I have. As you follow Christ, he will show you how your words can be life-giving.

People do a variety of things to deal with the problem of controlling their tongue. Some people choose to just keep their mouth shut. This is not a bad option because it keeps you from saying things you would regret later. Others say things and then try to retract them by saying, "I am sorry I said that. I really didn't mean it. I was just angry." Still others don't worry too much about it. They just say what's on their mind and they let others deal with it. They are proud that people say of them, "You always know where you stand with that person. He speaks his mind." Each of these has its benefits but none of these are the way of Jesus! Let's look at the passages you read today.

According to James 3:5–6, what does the tongue do?...

....

All three of the responses mentioned above are our attempts to tame our own tongue. *What does James 3:8 say about these approaches to the tongue?*...

....

According to Jesus' words in Matthew 12:33–35, what is the core issue?......................................

It really is a heart issue, isn't it? What comes out of you and me is what is really in us. If we follow Christ and devote our time and energy to allowing him to fill our hearts, our speech will follow because it's out of the overflow of the heart that our mouths speak. If your heart is full of godly things, when it overflows, good things will come out. If it is full of evil things, evil things will come out. Think of your tongue as a barometer of your heart. What you talk about and think about is what is important to you. Listen to yourself talk today. What kinds of things do you talk about? You may want to keep a notepad near you today to write down your thoughts and words. Your words will show you what you value and the condition of your soul. When you hear yourself saying something you think wouldn't glorify God, ask yourself why you are saying it. Is it because you want others to think of you a certain way? Are you trying to get someone to do something?

Allowing Jesus to transform your heart and your words is extremely important because Jesus says in Matthew 12:36–37 that we will have to give account one day for every word we said. We are responsible for our hearts and our words. That's a sobering thought! What better time than now to surrender your heart and words to the Lord?

What strategies does the Apostle Paul give in Ephesians 4:29–32 that could help you with your heart and words?..

....

....

Ultimately any change in your behavior is a result of your relationship with Christ bringing about that change. That being said, if you're going to honor Christ with your tongue, you have to make a determined effort in five ways:

1 ▹ Even though you can't tame your tongue, you can curb what you say that is hurtful (Ephesians 4:29). You have probably heard the saying, "If you don't have something good to say, don't say it." There is some truth to this. You can develop the habit of saying only good things about others because they too are wonderfully made and loved by God.

2 ▹ You need to acknowledge that it grieves the Holy Spirit when you say hurtful things about others (Ephesians 4:30). God loves everyone, and it hurts him when you talk poorly about the ones he created.

3 ▹ You must get rid of bitterness, rage, anger, brawling, slander and malice (Ephesians 4:31). Most of the time we say hurtful things about people who have hurt us. When you want to say something hurtful about someone, ask yourself how that person hurt you. When you identify that hurt, don't respond the way you used to, take it to the Lord! You may want to go back to Quality Six–Step 4 of this guide to remind yourself how to pray through pain. Let God carry the pain for you. Let it go. Get rid of it.

4 ▹ Be kind and compassionate to others just as Jesus modeled toward you and me (Ephesians 4:32). Regardless of how others treat you, you have control over your actions toward them. There's amazing freedom in knowing someone's actions do not dictate your responses. You can be kind and compassionate toward others because God is that way to you!

5 ▹ We all need forgiveness. The pathway to learning to love God with your words comes back to God's forgiveness for you. When you remember how much you needed and still need God to forgive you, it enables you to forgive others.

What would you like to do today to apply these principles to your life?..

....

Tell God in your own words what you would like him to help you with today. Be sure to thank him for what he has done in your life already.

....

....

....

....

....

NOTES

learn to MANAGE YOUR TIME

"______ ______ ______ ____ ________ _____ ____ ____________, _____ ____ ______ _______ ____ ___ ______ ___ _____ ___ _____." _________ __:__

"But seek first his kingdom and his righteousness, and all these things will be given to you as well." Matthew 6:33

SCRIPTURE

Read: Genesis 2:2–3; Exodus 20:8–11; Genesis 2:15; Psalm 90:12; Ecclesiastes 3

Leo Tolstoy wrote a famous story entitled, "How Much Land Does a Man Need?"[1] In it he describes an ambitious peasant named Pakhom, who heard about a country where he could have all the land he wanted for a thousand rubles. The only requirement was that he had to be able to walk around the entire plot in one day. Pakhom was quite confident that he could go far in one day. The rules were simple. He paid the thousand rubles upfront, would walk the entire property in one day, and then return to the starting point by sundown. If he did not get back to the starting point by sundown, the money and the land would be forfeited. In the story, Pakhom went too far in the early part of the day which resulted in his having to push himself especially hard to try to get back to the starting point. Near the end of the day the story describes him running with burning lungs, a sweat-soaked shirt and a parched throat. He did make it back to the starting point just in time and he collapsed.

Pakhom's worker ran to help him up only to discover he had died of exhaustion. The worker took Pakhom's shovel, dug a grave, and buried him on a six-foot piece of land, the exact amount of land a man needs.

Many of us are running ourselves ragged by living overloaded lives. Our lust for more is driving us to live beyond our limits, and it is resulting in exhaustion and burnout. God didn't design us to work or play all the time. He designed us to work hard for short seasons and then to rest and reflect. God set aside one day a week for rest and renewal.

Read Genesis 2:2–3 again. *Does it surprise you that God rested from his work? Why or why not?.....*

....

I believe God rested on the seventh day not because he was tired but to model for us that we need it. God's ways are always best but we don't always think so. Notice in Exodus 20:7–11 that taking a Sabbath (a day of rest) is one of the Ten Commandments. God requires it of his people. There is no age bracket given. A lot of people think that a day of rest is only needed by adults but that isn't biblical. Especially given the fast-paced society you live in: homework, part-time jobs, after-school activities and relationships are all pulling for your time.

Why do you think most Americans don't take a day to rest and reflect?..

Do you currently take a day to rest and reflect? Why or why not?...

...

Some people start obeying God in this area by taking a portion of a day to rest and reflect and then grow into it. Others just dive right in and take twenty-four hours.

Would you like to work towards taking a Sabbath (one day to rest) or a portion of a Sabbath? What day works for you?..

What kinds of things could you do on a Sabbath to help renew your spiritual, physical, and emotional being?...

...

What decisions would you need to make for that to happen?...

...

What will you have to give up in your current schedule to set yourself up for a balanced, fulfilling life?

...

Choosing not to work when you are able is equally dishonoring to God. Notice in Genesis 2:15 that God gave man work before the curse. In other words, work isn't part of the curse. Work is harder because of the curse but work is not the curse. This means it is God's will that you would embrace your work in life. The Bible describes those who do not work faithfully as "sluggards." At this point in your life, "work" is your schooling. Doing well in school creates opportunity for you to get the education you will need to provide for yourself and loved ones in the future. There are painful consequences for living the life of a sluggard which you will want to avoid.[2] The Apostle Paul wrote directly to men in 1 Timothy 5:8 about providing for their families, "If anyone does not provide for his relatives, and especially for his immediate family, he has denied the faith and is worse than an unbeliever."

Is working a problem for you? If so, what steps are you going to take to change this?........................

....

....

Learning to be a good manager of your time is all about balance, making sure you are taking care of the most important things first. A good start is to decide on and schedule times when you work and rest and reflect. We could have also talked about making time for important relationships, taking care of your body, etc. It's a process to learn how to use your time to honor God.

Are there other areas of your life that you need God's help with concerning your time?.....................

....

What needs to happen so you can take steps in the right direction?..

....

(You will want to share your decisions with your spiritual coach.)

Ask God to help you right now by praying Psalm 90:12 with the psalmist. *Lord, teach me to number my days, that I may gain a heart of wisdom. I want to please you with how I manage my time. Help me as I take steps today to be faithful with the time you have given me. I want to honor you and fulfill my purpose. I believe I can do that if you will help me and guide me. Amen.*

....

....

....

....

....

....

NOTES

learn to MANAGE YOUR GIFTS

MEMORIZE SCRIPTURE ▹

"____ ____ ____ ____ ________ ____ ____ ____________, ____ ____ ____ ____ ____

__ ____ __ ____ ____ ____." ________ __:__

"But seek first his kingdom and his righteousness, and all these things will be given to you as well." Matthew 6:33

Read: Ephesians 2:10; 1 Corinthians 12:7–11; 1 Peter 4:10–11; Matthew 25:14–30

It is an amazing thing to me that God allows us the privilege of joining with him to change the world. He could do everything himself, but he chooses to do some of his work through us. I am so humbled by that.

How does Ephesians 2:10 describe us?..

Why were we created?..

When did God prepare our work for us?..

You are not an accident or an evolution of nature. God had you in mind long before you were born. He designed you with specific spiritual gifts, passions, abilities, and a certain personality type so you could make a unique impact on the world that would bring him glory. Isn't that incredible? You may not know at this point what your unique contribution will be for God, but the Bible guarantees you that God has a plan for your life that's not like anyone else's.

Who does the Spirit give gifts to according to 1 Corinthians 12:7?.......................................

Why were these gifts given?.......................................

It's really important to realize the gifts God gives you aren't for you but for others. No one has all the gifts. That's why we need each other to become all that God wants us to become. When I do my part and you do yours, we can make an impact for God!

According to 1 Corinthians 12:11, who decides who receives which gifts?.......................................

How does 1 Peter 4:10 affect how you think about your gifts?.......................................

According to 1 Peter 4:11, what is the ultimate goal of your gifts?.......................................

I would not be telling you the whole truth if I didn't tell you there are huge implications for how you manage the gifts God has given you. Matthew 25:14–30 describes God's kingdom like a master who entrusted his property to his servants before he went on a journey. He gave each of them a different portion of his property (called "talents" in the story). When he returned, he expected each of them to have done something with the resources he gave them. Those who received five and two talents used them to gain even more. This pleased the master and he put them in charge of many things. But the servant who received only one talent and did nothing with it, received a harsh rebuke from the master. The master said, "You wicked, lazy servant." And the master took what he had given to that servant, and he gave it away to those who had done something with their resources. Then the master sent the servant out into the darkness where there was weeping and gnashing of teeth. This is a sobering parable but one we should take to heart as followers of Jesus. God invests heavily in each one of us because he has significant purposes for our lives. His purpose for your life is important. You matter! You only fail if you attempt nothing for God.

What gifts and resources has God given you?..

....

What would you like to do for God in line with those gifts and resources?...

....

What could you do with what God has given you to serve others?...

....

As we conclude *Learning to Follow Jesus: Youth Edition*, pray the prayer below and know that both of us (Daniel and Claude) are praying this prayer with you!

It amazes us, Heavenly Father, that you reach out to us to show us your kindness, to love us, to teach us, to befriend us, and to give us a meaningful life. It humbles us to realize that our lives matter so much to you. Help us to manage the gifts and resources you have given us in such a way that we fulfill what you had in mind when you created us. Help us to live today and each day hereafter for you alone. Thank you for giving our lives meaning. We belong to you! Amen.

COACH'S SECTION

Relate

How are you doing?

Review

How is your prayer life coming?

Have you been able to keep your quiet time consistent this week?

What did you learn in your prayer life this week?

Reflect

How did it go with the Learn to Manage quality?

What key areas stood out to you?

Refocus

What steps did you identify that you would like to take with putting God first in your finances?

How about with your body?

How is your time management?

Resource

In which of those areas would you like some support?

What do you need in order to get where you want to go in all of these areas?

Prayer

How can I pray for you this week?

Note: Turn to the prayer list you started for this person.

Ask if God has answered their requests from the previous week.

Pray for what they asked and that God would bless them in their next steps as a follower of Christ.

Note

Ask this person if he or she has been water baptized (by full immersion). If not, explain that water baptism is a public confession of his or her decision to follow Jesus. Assist him or her in taking that step, and provide opportunity for discussion and more information, if necessary.

Next Step

Review the "Next Step" Section on the following page.

....

....

....

....

....

PRAYER REQUESTS

Congratulations, you've been spiritually coached through the seven qualities of a Christ follower! Learning to follow Jesus is a lifelong journey of growing in each quality. Now that you've completed this book, what's next? The next step is to keep following! A good way to do that is by continuing your journey by spiritually coaching a friend or loved one with Daniel and Claude's book *Learning to Follow Jesus: Youth Edition*. Disciple-making is something we are all called to do. You may decide to be coached through this book again but be prayerfully considering whom the Lord may be asking you to spiritually coach.

As you know, this book provides practical, step-by-step guidance on your journey with Christ. Your spiritual coach was coached at one time, like you. Decide to continue following by bringing someone alongside you as you continue to learn to follow Jesus!

If you are interested in ordering additional *Learning to Follow Jesus: Youth Edition* books, you can order at: www.learningtofollow.net or you can contact the publisher, Morning Joy Media, whose information is located on the copyright page of this book.

Keep learning to follow Jesus and make disciples!

RESOURCES

GENERAL RESOURCES

Who Does God Say I Am?

- **I am a child of God.**
  Yet to all who received him, to those who believed in his name, he gave the right to become children of God. (John 1:12)
- **I am a branch of the true vine, and a conduit of Christ's life.**
  I am the true vine, and my Father is the gardener…I am the vine; you are the branches. If a man remains in me and I in him, he will bear much fruit; apart from me you can do nothing. (John 15:1, 5)
- **I am a friend of Jesus.**
  I no longer call you servants, because a servant does not know his master's business. Instead, I have called you friends, for everything that I learned from my Father I have made known to you. (John 15:15)
- **I am justified and redeemed.**
  This righteousness from God comes through faith in Jesus Christ to all who believe. There is no difference, for all have sinned and fall short of the glory of God, and are justified freely by his grace through the redemption that came by Christ Jesus. (Romans 3:22-24)
- **My old self was crucified with Christ, and I am no longer a slave to sin.**
  For we know that our old self was crucified with him so that the body of sin might be done away with, that we should no longer be slaves to sin—because anyone who has died has been freed from sin. (Romans 6:6-7)
- **God will not condemn me.**
  Therefore, there is now no condemnation for those who are in Christ Jesus... (Romans 8:1)
- **I am set free from the law of sin and death.**
  For through Christ Jesus the law of the Spirit of life set me free from the law of sin and death. (Romans 8:2)
- **As a child of God, I am a fellow heir with Christ.**
  Now if we are children, then we are heirs—heirs of God and co-heirs with Christ, if indeed we share in his sufferings in order that we may also share in his glory. (Romans 8:17)
- **Christ accepts me.**
  Accept one another, then, just as Christ accepted you, in order to bring praise to God. (Romans 15:7)

- **I am called to be a saint.**
  To the church of God in Corinth, to those sanctified in Christ Jesus and called to be holy, together with all those everywhere who call on the name of our Lord Jesus Christ—their Lord and ours. (1 Corinthians 1:2; see also Ephesians 1:1; Philippians 1:1; Colossians 1:2)
- **In Christ Jesus, I have wisdom, righteousness, sanctification, and redemption.**
  It is because of him that you are in Christ Jesus, who has become for us wisdom from God—that is, our righteousness, holiness and redemption. (1 Corinthians 1:30)
- **My body is the temple of the Holy Spirit, who dwells in me.**
  Don't you know that you yourselves are God's temple and that God's Spirit lives in you?...Do you not know that your body is a temple of the Holy Spirit, who is in you, whom you have received from God? You are not your own; you were bought at a price. Therefore honor God with your body. (1 Corinthians 3:16; 6:19–20)
- **I am joined to the Lord and am one in spirit with him.**
  But he who unites himself with the Lord is one with him in spirit. (1 Corinthians 6:17)
- **God leads me in the triumph and knowledge of Christ.**
  But thanks be to God, who always leads us in triumphal procession in Christ and through us spreads everywhere the fragrance of the knowledge of him. (2 Corinthians 2:14)
- **The hardening of my mind has been removed in Christ.**
  But their minds were made dull, for to this day the same veil remains when the old covenant is read. It has not been removed, because only in Christ is it taken away. (2 Corinthians 3:14)
- **I am a new creature in Christ.**
  Therefore, if anyone is in Christ, he is a new creation; the old has gone, the new has come! (2 Corinthians 5:17)
- **I have become the righteousness of God in Christ.**
  God made him who had no sin to be sin for us, so that in him we might become the righteousness of God. (2 Corinthians 5:21)
- **I have been made one with all who are in Christ Jesus.**
  There is neither Jew nor Greek, slave nor free, male nor female, for you are all one in Christ Jesus. (Galatians 3:28)
- **I am no longer a slave but a child and an heir.**
  So you are no longer a slave, but a son; and since you are a son, God has made you also an heir. (Galatians 4:7)
- **I have been set free in Christ.**
  It is for freedom that Christ has set us free. Stand firm, then, and do not let yourselves be burdened again by a yoke of slavery. (Galatians 5:1)

("Who Does God Say I Am?" continued...)

- **I have been blessed with every spiritual blessing in the heavenly places.**
  Praise be to the God and Father of our Lord Jesus Christ, who has blessed us in the heavenly realms with every spiritual blessing in Christ. (Ephesians 1:3)
- **I am chosen, holy, and blameless before God.**
  For he chose us in him before the creation of the world to be holy and blameless in his sight. (Ephesians 1:4)
- **I am redeemed and forgiven by the grace of Christ.**
  In him we have redemption through his blood, the forgiveness of sins, in accordance with the riches of God's grace... (Ephesians 1:7)
- **I have been predestined by God to obtain an inheritance.**
  To be put into effect when the times will have reached their fulfillment—to bring all things in heaven and on earth together under one head, even Christ. In him we were also chosen, having been predestined according to the plan of him who works out everything in conformity with the purpose of his will... (Ephesians 1:10-11)
- **I have been sealed with the Holy Spirit of promise.**
  And you also were included in Christ when you heard the word of truth, the gospel of your salvation. Having believed, you were marked in him with a seal, the promised Holy Spirit... (Ephesians 1:13)
- **Because of God's mercy and love, I have been made alive with Christ.**
  But because of his great love for us, God, who is rich in mercy, made us alive with Christ even when we were dead in transgressions—it is by grace you have been saved. (Ephesians 2:4-5)
- **I am seated in the heavenly places with Christ.**
  And God raised us up with Christ and seated us with him in the heavenly realms in Christ Jesus. (Ephesians 2:6)
- **I am God's workmanship created to produce good works.**
  For we are God's workmanship, created in Christ Jesus to do good works, which God prepared in advance for us to do. (Ephesians 2:10)
- **I have been brought near to God by the blood of Christ.**
  But now in Christ Jesus you who once were far away have been brought near through the blood of Christ. (Ephesians 2:13)
- **I am a member of Christ's body and a partaker of his promise.**
  This mystery is that through the gospel the Gentiles are heirs together with Israel, members together of one body, and sharers together in the promise in Christ Jesus... for we are members of his body. (Ephesians 3:6; 5:30)
- **I have boldness and confident access to God through faith in Christ.**
  In him and through faith in him we may approach God with freedom and confidence. (Ephesians 3:12)

- **My new self is righteous and holy.**
  Put on the new self, created to be like God in true righteousness and holiness. (Ephesians 4:24)
- **I was formerly darkness, but now I am light in the Lord.**
  For you were once darkness, but now you are light in the Lord. Live as children of light. (Ephesians 5:8)
- **I am a citizen of heaven.**
  But our citizenship is in heaven. And we eagerly await a Savior from there, the Lord Jesus Christ. (Philippians 3:20)
- **The peace of God guards my heart and mind.**
  And the peace of God, which transcends all understanding, will guard your hearts and your minds in Christ Jesus. (Philippians 4:7)
- **God supplies all my needs.**
  And my God will meet all your needs according to his glorious riches in Christ Jesus. (Philippians 4:19)
- **I have been made complete in Christ.**
  You have been given fullness in Christ, who is the head over every power and authority. (Colossians 2:10)
- **I have been raised with Christ.**
  Since, then, you have been raised with Christ, set your hearts on things above, where Christ is seated at the right hand of God. (Colossians 3:1)
- **My life is hidden with Christ in God.**
  For you died, and your life is now hidden with Christ in God. (Colossians 3:3)
- **Christ is my life, and I will be revealed with him in glory.**
  When Christ, who is your life, appears, then you also will appear with him in glory. (Colossians 3:4)
- **I have been chosen of God, and I am holy and beloved.**
  Therefore, as God's chosen people, holy and dearly loved, clothe yourselves with compassion, kindness, humility, gentleness and patience. (Colossians 3:12)
- **God loves me and has chosen me.**
  For we know, brothers loved by God, that he has chosen you. (1 Thessalonians 1:4)

Scripture Memory Summary

From *First Steps: Youth Edition*—Matthew 4:19
"Come, follow me," Jesus said, "and I will make you fishers of men."

Quality 1 ▹ Learn to Be With Jesus—Matthew 11:28–30
28 "Come to me, all you who are weary and burdened, and I will give you rest. 29 Take my yoke upon you and learn
from me, for I am gentle and humble in heart, and you will find rest for your souls. 30 For my yoke is easy and my
burden is light."

Quality 2 ▹ Learn to Listen—Matthew 7:24–25
24 "Therefore everyone who hears these words of mine and puts them into practice is like a wise man who built
his house on the rock. 25 The rain came down, the streams rose, and the winds blew and beat against that house;
yet it did not fall, because it had its foundation on the rock."

Quality 3 ▹ Learn to Heal—Matthew 7:7–8
7 "Ask and it will be given to you; seek and you will find; knock and the door will be opened to you. 8 For everyone
who asks receives; he who seeks finds; and to him who knocks, the door will be opened."

Quality 4 ▹ Learn to Influence—Matthew 28:18–20
18 Then Jesus came to them and said, "All authority in heaven and on earth has been given to me. 19 Therefore go
and make disciples of all nations, baptizing them in the name of the Father and of the Son and of the Holy Spirit,
20 and teaching them to obey everything I have commanded you. And surely I am with you always, to the very end
of the age."

Quality 5 ▹ Learn to Love—Matthew 22:37–39
37 Jesus replied: "'Love the Lord your God with all your heart and with all your soul and with all your mind.' 38 This
is the first and greatest commandment. 39 And the second is like it: 'Love your neighbor as yourself.'"

Quality 6 ▹ Learn to Pray—Matthew 6:9–13
9 "This, then, is how you should pray: 'Our Father in heaven, hallowed be your name, 10 your kingdom come, your
will be done on earth as it is in heaven. 11 Give us today our daily bread. 12 Forgive us our debts, as we also have
forgiven our debtors. 13 And lead us not into temptation, but deliver us from the evil one.'"

Quality 7 ▹ Learn to Manage—Matthew 6:33
33 "But seek first his kingdom and his righteousness, and all these things will be given to you as well."

(Additional "Challenge Memory Verses" on next page...)

Challenge Memory Verses

From *First Steps: Youth Edition*
Proverbs 3:5–6
5 Trust in the Lord with all your heart and lean not on your own understanding; 6 in all your ways acknowledge him,
and he will make your paths straight.

Jeremiah 29:11
11 "For I know the plans I have for you," declares the Lord, "plans to prosper you and not to harm you, plans to
give you hope and a future."

Quality 1 ▹ Learn to Be With Jesus
John 15:5
5 "I am the vine; you are the branches. If a man remains in me and I in him, he will bear much fruit; apart from me
you can do nothing."

Matthew 16:24–25
24 Then Jesus said to his disciples, "If anyone would come after me, he must deny himself and take up his cross
and follow me. 25 For whoever wants to save his life will lose it, but whoever loses his life for me will find it."

Galatians 2:20
20 I have been crucified with Christ and I no longer live, but Christ lives in me. The life I live in the body, I live by
faith in the Son of God, who loved me and gave himself for me.

1 John 1:8–10
8 If we claim to be without sin, we deceive ourselves and the truth is not in us. 9 If we confess our sins, he is faithful and just and will forgive us our sins and purify us from all unrighteousness. 10 If we claim we have not sinned,
we make him out to be a liar and his word has no place in our lives.

Quality 2 ▹ Learn to Listen
John 10:27
27 My sheep listen to my voice; I know them, and they follow me.

2 Timothy 3:16–17
16 All Scripture is God-breathed and is useful for teaching, rebuking, correcting and training in righteousness, 17
so that the man of God may be thoroughly equipped for every good work.

Psalm 119:11
11 I have hidden your word in my heart that I might not sin against you.

Psalm 119:105
105 Your word is a lamp to my feet and a light for my path.

1 Corinthians 10:13
13 No temptation has seized you except what is common to man. And God is faithful; he will not let you be tempted beyond what you can bear. But when you are tempted, he will also provide a way out so that you can stand up under it.

Luke 6:46
46 “Why do you call me, ‘Lord, Lord,’ and do not do what I say?”

Quality 3 ▸ Learn to Heal

Jeremiah 32:27
27 “I am the Lord, the God of all mankind. Is anything too hard for me?”

2 Corinthians 1:3–4
3 Praise be to the God and Father of our Lord Jesus Christ, the Father of compassion and the God of all comfort,
4 who comforts us in all our troubles, so that we can comfort those in any trouble with the comfort we ourselves
have received from God.

Psalm 103:2–5
2 Praise the Lord, O my soul, and forget not all his benefits— 3 who forgives all your sins and heals all your
diseases, 4 who redeems your life from the pit and crowns you with love and compassion, 5 who satisfies your
desires with good things so that your youth is renewed like the eagle’s.

(Quality 3 verses continued...)

1 Peter 2:24
24 He himself bore our sins in his body on the tree, so that we might die to sins and live for righteousness; by his
wounds you have been healed.

Quality 4 ▹ Learn to Influence

Acts 1:8
8 "But you will receive power when the Holy Spirit comes on you; and you will be my witnesses in Jerusalem, and
in all Judea and Samaria, and to the ends of the earth."

John 3:16–17
16 "For God so loved the world that he gave his one and only Son, that whoever believes in him shall not perish
but have eternal life. 17 For God did not send his Son into the world to condemn the world, but to save the world
through him."

Ephesians 2:8–10
8 For it is by grace you have been saved, through faith—and this not from yourselves, it is the gift of God— 9 not
by works, so that no one can boast. 10 For we are God's workmanship, created in Christ Jesus to do good works,
which God prepared in advance for us to do.

Luke 19:10
10 "For the Son of Man came to seek and to save what was lost."

2 Peter 3:9
9 The Lord is not slow in keeping his promise, as some understand slowness. He is patient with you, not wanting
anyone to perish, but everyone to come to repentance.

Mark 10:45
45 For even the Son of Man did not come to be served, but to serve, and to give his life as a ransom for many."

1 John 5:11–12
11 And this is the testimony: God has given us eternal life, and this life is in his Son. 12 He who has the Son has life;
he who does not have the Son of God does not have life.

Romans 10:14–15
[14] How, then, can they call on the one they have not believed in? And how can they believe in the one of whom they have not heard? And how can they hear without someone preaching to them? [15] And how can they preach unless they are sent? As it is written, "How beautiful are the feet of those who bring good news!"

Quality 5 ▹ Learn to Love

2 Corinthians 5:17
[17] Therefore, if anyone is in Christ, he is a new creation; the old has gone, the new has come!

Psalm 37:4–6
[4] Delight yourself in the Lord and he will give you the desires of your heart. [5] Commit your way to the Lord; trust in him and he will do this: [6] He will make your righteousness shine like the dawn, the justice of your cause like the noonday sun.

Philippians 4:4–7
[4] Rejoice in the Lord always. I will say it again: Rejoice! [5] Let your gentleness be evident to all. The Lord is near.
[6] Do not be anxious about anything, but in everything, by prayer and petition, with thanksgiving, present your requests to God. [7] And the peace of God, which transcends all understanding, will guard your hearts and your minds in Christ Jesus.

Lamentations 3:22–25
[22] Because of the Lord's great love we are not consumed, for his compassions never fail. [23] They are new every morning; great is your faithfulness. [24] I say to myself, "The Lord is my portion; therefore I will wait for him." [25] The Lord is good to those whose hope is in him, to the one who seeks him.

Quality 6 ▹ Learn to Pray

Ephesians 6:18
[18] And pray in the Spirit on all occasions with all kinds of prayers and requests. With this in mind, be alert and always keep on praying for all the saints.

(Quality 6 verses continued...)

1 Timothy 2:1–2
[1] I urge, then, first of all, that requests, prayers, intercession and thanksgiving be made for everyone— [2] for kings
and all those in authority, that we may live peaceful and quiet lives in all godliness and holiness.

Jeremiah 33:3
[3] 'Call to me and I will answer you and tell you great and unsearchable things you do not know.'

Isaiah 55:8–11
[8] "For my thoughts are not your thoughts, neither are your ways my ways," declares the Lord. [9] "As the heavens
are higher than the earth, so are my ways higher than your ways and my thoughts than your thoughts. [10] As the
rain and the snow come down from heaven, and do not return to it without watering the earth and making it bud
and flourish, so that it yields seed for the sower and bread for the eater, [11] so is my word that goes out from
my mouth: It will not return to me empty, but will accomplish what I desire and achieve the purpose for which I
sent it."

John 15:7–8
[7] If you remain in me and my words remain in you, ask whatever you wish, and it will be given you. [8] This is to my
Father's glory, that you bear much fruit, showing yourselves to be my disciples.

Quality 7 ▹ Learn to Manage

Matthew 6:19–21
[19] "Do not store up for yourselves treasures on earth, where moth and rust destroy, and where thieves break in
and steal. [20] But store up for yourselves treasures in heaven, where moth and rust do not destroy, and where
thieves do not break in and steal. [21] For where your treasure is, there your heart will be also."

Proverbs 16:3
[3]Commit to the Lord whatever you do, and your plans will succeed.

Proverbs 3:9–10
[9] Honor the Lord with your wealth, with the firstfruits of all your crops; [10] then your barns will be filled to overflow-
ing, and your vats will brim over with new wine.

Titus 1:7–9
7 Since an overseer is entrusted with God's work, he must be blameless—not overbearing, not quick-tempered,
not given to drunkenness, not violent, not pursuing dishonest gain. 8 Rather he must be hospitable, one who loves
what is good, who is self-controlled, upright, holy and disciplined. 9 He must hold firmly to the trustworthy message as it has been taught, so that he can encourage others by sound doctrine and refute those who oppose it.

Selected Bibliography

* Indicates the recommended first book to read on a quality.

Quality 1 ▹ Learn to Be With Jesus

Barton, Ruth Haley. *Sacred Rhythms: Arranging Our Lives for Spiritual Transformation.* InterVarsity, 2006.

Blackaby, Henry, Richard Blackaby, and Claude King. *Experiencing God,* rev.ed. Nashville: Broadman & Holman, 2008.

Bonhoeffer, Dietrich. *Life Together.* New York: Harper and Row, 1976.

———. *The Cost of Discipleship.* Riverside, NJ: MacMillan Publishing, 1967.

Brother Lawrence, *The Practice of the Presence of God.* New York: Doubleday, 1977.

*Foster, Richard. *Celebration of Discipline.* San Francisco: Harper, 1988.

Law, William. *A Serious Call to a Devout and Holy Life.* Philadelphia: Westminster, 1955.

Merton, Thomas. *Contemplative Prayer.* Garden City, NY: Doubleday and Co., 1971.

Murray, Andrew. *Abide in Christ.* New York: Whitaker House, 2002.

Sheldon, Charles. *In His Steps.* Nashville, TN: Broadman, 1935.

Smith, Gordon T. *The Voice of Jesus: Discernment, Prayer, and the Witness of the Spirit.* Downers Grove, IL: InterVarsity, 2003.

Willard, Dallas. *Spirit of the Disciplines.* San Francisco: Harper and Row, 1991 (1990).

Quality 2 ▹ Learn to Listen

Chamber, Oswald. *My Utmost for His Highest.* New York: Mead, 1935.

*Fee, Gordon and Douglas Stuart. *How to Read the Bible for All Its Worth.* Grand Rapids: Zondervan, 2003.

Hendricks, Howard G. and William D. Hendricks, *Living By the Book.* Chicago: Moody, 1991.

Quality 3 ▸ Learn to Heal

Anderson, Neil. *The Bondage Breaker.* Eugene, OR: Harvest House Publishers, 1993.

Baker, John. *Life's Healing Choices: Freedom from Your Hurts, Hang-ups, and Habits.* New York: Howard Books, 2007.

Bosworth, F. F. *Christ the Healer.* Old Tappan, NJ: Fleming, 1973.

Cloud, Henry and John Townsend. *Boundaries.* Grand Rapids: Zondervan, 1992.

*Richards, James. *How to Stop the Pain.* New Kensington, PA: Whitaker House, 2001.

Sande, Ken. *The Peace Maker.* Grand Rapids: Baker, 2004.

Seamands, David A. *Healing for Damaged Emotions.* Colorado Springs: David C. Cook, 1981.

Quality 4 ▸ Learn to Influence

Aldrich, Joe. *Life-Style Evangelism.* Sisters, OR: Multnomah, 2006.

Carnegie, Dale. *How to Win Friends & Influence People.* New York: Pocket Books, 1936.

Cox, Harvey. *Fire from Heaven.* New York: Addison-Wesley, 1995.

Deere, Jack. *Surprised By the Power of the Spirit.* Grand Rapids: Zondervan, 1993.

Egli, Jim and Ben Hoerr. *The I-Factor.* Houston: Touch Publications, 1993.

Fee, Gordon. *God's Empowering Presence.* Peabody, MA: Hendrickson, 1994.

Ford, Leighton. *Good News Is for Sharing.* Elgin, IL: David C. Cook, 1977.

Greenfield, John. *Power from on High.* Muskegon, MI: Dust to Ashes Publications, 1996.

Gumbel, Nicky. *Questions of Life.* Colorado Springs: David C. Cook, 2004.

Hurst, Randy. *The Helper.* Springfield, MO: Gospel Publishing House, 2004.

*Hybels, Bill and Mark Middelberg. *Becoming a Contagious Christian.* Grand Rapids: Eerdmans, 1994.

Kinnaman, David and Gabe Lyons. *UnChristian.* Grand Rapids: Baker, 2007.

Lewis, C. S. *Mere Christianity.* New York: Macmillan, 1960.

Little, Paul. *Know Why You Believe.* Wheaton: Victor Books, 1974.

———. *How to Give Away Your Faith.* Downers Grove, IL: InterVarsity Press, 1988.

McDowell, Josh. *More Than a Carpenter.* Wheaton: Tyndale, 1977.

(Selected Bibliography continued...)

resources

McLaren, Brian. *Finding Faith.* Grand Rapids: Zondervan, 2007.
———. *More Ready Than You Realize.* Grand Rapids: Zondervan, 2002.
Menzies, William W. and Robert P. Menzies. *Spirit and Power.* Grand Rapids: Zondervan, 2000.
Nouwen, Henri. *In the Name of Jesus.* New York: Crossroads Publishing Company, 1992.
Pippert, Rebecca Manley. *Out of the Salt Shaker and Into the World.* Downers Grove, IL: InterVarsity Press, 1979.
Sherrill, John L. *They Speak with Other Tongues.* New York: Jove, 1964.
Strobel, Lee. *A Case for a Creator.* Grand Rapids: Zondervan, 2004.
———. *A Case For Christ.* Grand Rapids: Zondervan, 1998.
———. *A Case For Faith.* Grand Rapids: Zondervan, 2000.
Wood, George O. *Living in the Spirit.* Springfield, MO: 2009.

Quality 5 ▹ Learn to Love

Crabb, Larry. *Finding God.* Grand Rapids: Zondervan, 1993.
* McGee, Robert. *The Search for Significance.* Houston: Rapha Publishing, 1990.
Mahaney, C. J. *The Cross Centered Life.* Sisters, OR: Multnomah, 2002.
Packer, J. I. *Knowing God.* Downers Grove, IL: InterVarsity Press, 1973.

Quality 6 ▹ Learn to Pray

Batterson, Mark. *The Circle Maker: Praying Circles Around Your Biggest Dreams and Greatest Fears.* Grand Rapids: Zondervan, 2011.
Bounds, E.M. *A Treasury of Prayer.* Minneapolis: Bethany Fellowship, Inc., 1960.
Eastman, Dick. *The Hour That Changes the World.* Grand Rapids: Baker, 1978.
Foster, Richard J. *Prayer.* San Francisco: Harper, 1992.
Grubb, Norman P. *Rees Howells Intercessor.* Philadelphia: Christian Literature Crusade, 1952.
* Hybels, Bill. *Too Busy Not To Pray.* Downers Grove: InterVarsity Press, 1988.
Murray, Andrew. *With Christ in the School of Prayer.* Philadelphia: H. Altemus, 1895.
Yancey, Philip. *Prayer: Does It Make Any Difference?* Grand Rapids: Zondervan, 2006.

Quality 7 ▹ Learn to Manage

Carnegie, Dale. *How to Win Friends & Influence People.* New York: Pocket Books, 1936.

Covey, Stephen. *The 7 Habits of Highly Effective People.* New York: Simon & Schuster, 1989.

Duncan, Todd. *Time Traps.* Nashville: Thomas Nelson, 2004.

*MacDonald, Gordon. *Ordering Your Private World.* Nashville: Thomas Nelson, 1984.

Maxwell, John C. *Developing the Leader Within You.* Nashville: Thomas Nelson, 1993.

———. *The Winning Attitude.* Nashville: Thomas Nelson, 1993.

Ramsey, Dave. *Total Money Makeover.* Nashville: Thomas Nelson, 2007.

Smith, Hyrum W. *The 10 Natural Laws of Successful Time and Life Management.* New York: Warner Brothers, 1994.

Swenson, Richard A. *Margin: Restoring Emotional, Physical, Financial, and Time Reserves to Overloaded Lives.* Colorado Springs: NavPress, 1992.

———. *The Overload Syndrome: Learning to Live Within Your Limits.* Colorado Springs: NavPress, 1998.

Winston, Stephanie. *Getting Organized.* New York: Grand Central Publishing, 2006.

www.mypyramid.gov

What Is a Spiritual Coach?

A spiritual coach is one who comes alongside another person to help him or her become an authentic follower of Christ.

Coming Alongside

You are on the journey with the person. You are not over the person.

Assume an attitude of humility. We are all learning to follow Jesus.

Helping

You are there to help. You won't have all the answers.

The focus is on the person being coached and not the coach.

Authentic Follower of Christ

The goal is that the other person will be an authentic follower of Jesus.

The goal is not completion of material—it's growing in the seven qualities of the follower of Jesus.

What is the Role of a Spiritual Coach?

To help the person continue to move along the path to following Christ (Hebrews 10:24, "And let us consider how we may spur one another on toward love and good deeds.")

To gently challenge a person to become an authentic follower of Jesus (Proverbs 27:17, "As iron sharpens iron, so one man sharpens another.")

What is the Process of Spiritual Coaching?[1]

Relate: establish coaching relationship and agenda

Reflect: discover and explore key issues

Refocus: determine priorities and action steps

Resource: provide support and encouragement

Review: evaluate, celebrate, and revise plans

What Types of Questions Will I Ask as a Spiritual Coach?

Relate: How are you doing? How was your week?

Reflect: What stood out to you this week in your reading? What obstacles are you facing?

Refocus: What would you like to do? What are some possible ways to get there?

Resource: What resources do you have? What resources are you missing? Would you like some accountability around that?

Review: What's working? What's not working? What needs to change?

Also, feel free to discuss the questions and action steps in which the student is encouraged to share his or her response with you. Do this whenever it feels appropriate during the coaching session.

Quality One ▸ Step Three

1. Some find once they become followers of Jesus, they are very hungry to read God's Word. If you are up for the challenge, you can read through the entire Bible in one year by reading about twenty minutes per day. Explore options that work for you at www.youversion.com.

Quality Two ▸ Step One

1. Haddon Robinson, *What Jesus Said About Successful Living* (Grand Rapids: Discovery House Publishers, 1991), 28.
2. Ibid.

Quality Two ▸ Step Four

1. If you found Deuteronomy 6:16, you are correct.

Quality Three ▸ Step One

1. http://www.time.com/time/magazine/article/0,9171,982784-1,00.html.

Quality Three ▸ Step Five

1. I recommend *When God Doesn't Make Sense* (Wheaton: Tyndale House Publishers, 1997) by James Dobson and *Where Is God When It Hurts* (Grand Rapids: Zondervan, 1990) by Philip Yancey.

Quality Three ▸ Resources

1. David H. Olson, *Prepare/Enrich Counselor's Manual* (Minneapolis: Life Innovations, Inc, 1982, 1986, 1996), 63–64.
2. Elisabeth Kubler-Ross and David Kessler, *On Grief and Grieving: Finding the Meaning of Grief Through the Five Stages of Loss* (New York: Scribner, 2005).
3. http://www.celebraterecovery.com.

Quality Four ▸ Introduction

1. Unfortunately different groups have had opposing views about speaking in tongues. Some make "speaking in tongues" the point of the baptism in the Holy Spirit. However, a simple reading of Acts 1:8 shows otherwise. Speaking in tongues was the normal part of that experience but not the goal. The experience repeating throughout the New Testament (Acts 10, 19; 1 Corinthians 12–14) shows it was a normal part of the early church and the expected experience. The purpose of the empowerment of the Spirit is to enable people to effectively witness for Christ. Others argue the experience isn't for the Christian today and some would say it should be avoided. A plain reading of Scripture shows that empowerment for witnessing was the focus of the experience. The division in the church worldwide

about the issue of speaking in tongues doesn't honor Jesus. Speaking in tongues is neither a spiritual badge to be worn with pride nor an experience that should be avoided. It's a blessing and a by-product of the empowerment of the Holy Spirit.

Quality Four ▸ Step One

1. Win and Charles Arn surveyed 14,000 people nationwide to ask them, "What or who was responsible for your coming to Christ?" At least 75 percent of respondents in every context said a friend or a family member was the most significant influence.
2. http://www.barna.org/barna-update/article/5-barna-update/196-evangelism-is-most-effective-among-kids.
3. 80 percent of the people surveyed by Thom Rainer indicated that they would attend a church if they were asked (*The UnChurched Next Door,* Grand Rapids: Zondervan, 2008), 32.

Quality Four ▸ Resources

1. Taken from *Becoming a Contagious Christian: Youth Edition* by LEE P. STROBEL; BILL HYBELS; MARK MITTELBERG; BO BOSHERS. Copyright © 2001 by Willow Creek Association. Used by permission of Zondervan. WWW.ZONDERVAN.COM.

Quality Five ▸ Step Two

1. Robert McGee, *The Search for Significance* (Houston: Rapha Publishing, 1985), 162

Quality Five ▸ Step Three

1. Robert S. McGee, *The Search for Significance*, 84
2. Ibid., 85.

Quality Five ▸ Step Four

1. Robert McGee, *The Search for Significance*, 108-110.

Quality Five ▸ Resources

1. Robert S. McGee, *The Search for Significance* (Houston: Rapha Publishing, 1985), 46–47. Used by permission.
2. Ibid., 66–67.
3. Ibid., 90–91.
4. Ibid., 105–106.
5. Ibid., 40–41.

Quality Six ▸ Introduction

1. The address of Maralyn's blog is http://www.maralynsupdates.blogspot.com.

(Notes continued...)

Quality Six ▸ Step Two

1. Tim Hughes. "Here I am to Worship" (Thankyou Music. Admin. by EMI Christian Music Publishing, 2000).
2. Chris Tomlin, Ed Cash, Jesse Reeves. "How Great is Our God" (worshiptogether.com songs. sixsteps Music. Alletrop Music. Admin. by EMI Christian Music Publishing, 2004).
3. Marty Sampson. "For Who You Are" (Hillsong Music Publishing. Admin. by EMI Christian Music Publishing, 2006).
4. Ben Fielding, Reuben Morgan. "God is Able" (Hillsong Music Publishing. Admin. by EMI Christian Music Publishing, 2010).
5. Chris Tomlin, Jesse Reeves, Jonas Myrin, Matt Redman. "Our God" (Thankyou Music. sixsteps Music. Said And Done Music. Vamos Publishing. SHOUT! Music Publishing. worshiptogether.com songs. Admin. by EMI Christian Music Publishing, 2010).

Quality Six ▸ Step Four

1. There are more than sixty lament psalms. There are individual laments (e.g. 3, 22, 31, 42, 57, 69, 71, 120, 139, and 142) and corporate laments (e.g. 12, 44, 80, 94, and 137). The lament usually exhibits the following pattern: Address the LORD; Complain; statement of Trust in the LORD; expectation of Deliverance; Assurance of the LORD's victory; and Praise for the LORD (Gordon Fee and Douglas Stewart, *How to Read the Bible for All Its Worth* [Grand Rapids: Zondervan, 2003]).

Quality Six ▸ Step Five

1. Martha Raddatz, *The Long Road Home* (New York: G. P. Putnam's Sons, 2007).

Quality Seven ▸ Step One

1. Walter F. Arndt and F. Wilbur Gingrich, *A Greek-English Lexicon of the New Testament* (Chicago: The University of Chicago Press, 1979), 475.
2. I (Daniel) am not sure to whom this quote belongs. It has been attributed to Ralph Waldo Emerson (1803–1882), Charles Reade (1814–1884), and a Buddist Proverb.

Quality Seven ▸ Step Two

1. This was discussed in *First Steps: Youth Edition*, in the overview of Quality Seven.
2. www.crown.org and www.daveramsey.com are good places to start.

Quality Seven ▸ Step Five

1. I (Daniel) first heard about this story in Richard Swenson's book, *The Overload Syndrome* (Colorado Springs: NavPress, 1998), 23–24.
2. Proverbs 6:6–11, 10:26, 13:4, 15:19, 19:24, 20:4, 21:25–26, 22:13, 24:30–34, 26:13–16.

Spiritual Coaching Resources

1. The coaching model adopted in this resource, particularly the 5Rs of coaching, comes from *Coaching 101* by Robert E. Logan, Sherilyn Carlton, and Tara Miller (ChurchSmart Resources, 2003). Used by permission.

SCRIPTURE REFERENCE INDEX

(Scripture Reference Index continued...)

(Topical Index continued...)